Oh, how I wish I had read this book when I [...] helped me to understand the emotions dri[...] helped me to build a solid financial footing from the beginning of my career. Pegues offers proven pathways for establishing habits that lead to wealth and well-being. I was encouraged by her stories of women navigating their careers by putting their best selves forward and stepping into opportunities.

Jacquelline Fuller, VP, Google; president, Google.org

Fifteen years ago, I sat in a crowded room and heard Deborah Pegues speak. All these years later, the principles she communicated and the truth she unfolded are still cemented in my heart and mind. This is what happens when Deborah teaches—lessons are learned, minds are renewed, ambitions are reshaped, and life trajectories are changed. The book you hold in your hands is an invitation—an opportunity to experience the practical, life-transforming gift of Deborah's expertise. Don't just read this. Savor it. Digest it. And then implement its principles as quickly as you can. Your finances and your future will thank you for it.

Priscilla Shirer, Bible teacher, author of *Fervent: A Woman's Battle Plan for Serious, Specific and Strategic Prayer*

Deborah has a unique, God-given ability to take the mystery and confusion out of financial jargon and concepts—and make them comprehensible. The practical wisdom featured in this book will surely equip women worldwide with the tools to handle their finances with confidence, excellence, and godly motivation. I highly recommend this timely and relevant resource.

Dr. Barbara McCoo Lewis, general supervisor, Church of God in Christ International, Inc., Department of Women

I wish I had been privileged to have this information seven decades ago. By the grace of God, I have done well. However, I would have been informed for greater financial success knowing and practicing the truths that Deborah is teaching in this powerful mentoring book. She highlights key money management do's and don'ts from the voice of the "Master Financier." Applying the principles of these truths will result in financial sensibility and stability for the rest of your life and for generations to come.

Thelma Wells, *Women of Faith* speaker, radio and TV host, author of *God Is Not Through with You Yet*, and president of A Woman of God Ministries

If anyone can talk to you about ████ ████ Deborah Pegues can! Based on her vast experience in handling the f████es of major corporations, ministries, and nonprofits, she delivers information you can bank on. God gives the power to gain wealth, and Deborah empowers you to manage it. A must read!

Michelle McKinney Hammond, TV host,
singer/songwriter, and author of *Divanomics*

Wiser about money in *one minute*? Yes! Deborah has kicked the door of opportunity wide for women to gain a better understanding of managing their finances.

Pam Farrel, bestselling coauthor of
Men Are Like Waffles, Women Are Like Spaghetti

The One-Minute Money Mentor for Women is life changing. We all know money is essential, but how we allow it to affect our lives is linked to our emotional health. If we're to break free, we must examine our souls because our financial situation is ultimately a spiritual issue.

Kathleen Cooke, cofounder of Cooke Pictures and
The Influence Lab and author of *Hope 4 Today*

Filled with practical wisdom, concise, and accessible, T*he One-Minute Money Mentor for Women* is for everyone, regardless of their financial failures or successes! Read it and buy copies for your friends and they'll be forever grateful!

Sarah Bowling, TV cohost, *Today with Marilyn and Sarah*, founder
of the Saving Moses Project, and author of *Heavenly Help*

Leave it to Deborah to take two subjects I hated in school, math and accounting, and make them easy and entertaining. She has a beautiful gift to comfort and correct. Thank you, Deborah!

P.B. (Bunny) Wilson, author, *Liberated Through Submission*
and *Your Knight in Shining Armor*

The One-Minute Money Mentor for Women will flip your financial world upside down. In this powerful book, Deborah masterfully helps you comprehend where you are and then step by step leads you to the place of financial peace. Every woman, whether she thinks her finances are in order or acknowledges they are a train wreck, needs to read this book.

Tracey Mitchell, author, *Downside Up*; TV host, *Life from DFW*;
and CEO of The Winning Woman Consulting Group

As a financial counselor for the past 20 years, I've observed many smart women who have made unwise financial decisions due to their lack of understanding of financial concepts, their attachment to toxic relationships, or a general mindset about finances that limits their dreams and goals. In her trademark direct and uncompromising style, Deborah confronts these and other pitfalls with no holds barred. I highly recommend this book to my clients and women everywhere.

> **George B. Thompson,** founder/president, Thompson Wealth
> Management and author of *The Wealth Cycle*

Every married woman whose husband handles their finances should read this book. I know firsthand the importance of being knowledgeable and equipped to step in and manage this crucial area when life's circumstances dictate. Deborah addresses such delicate financial situations with sensitivity and strong admonitions. Read this book and be prepared!

> **Patricia Ashley,** founder/CEO, Patricia Ashley Ministries and
> author of *Marriage Is a Blessing When It's Done God's Way*

I must admit that my greatest area of weakness is managing money. Deborah's book, *The One-Minute Money Mentor for Women*, gives me the tools I need to simplify my struggle in this area.

> **Terri McFaddin-Solomon,** author, speaker, two-time
> Grammy Award-winning songwriter, and cowriter of
> theme songs to movies *Men in Black* and *Big*

Deborah Pegues is teaching the new generation of women how we can be successful with our finances by providing practical and helpful tools we can all use. This book will transform your attitude toward money and improve your financial situation. I highly recommend it to any person who wants to get and keep their financial house in order!

> **Donna Recinos Clayton,** network director,
> TBN Salsa Network and TV host of *Faith with Flavor*

THE ONE-MINUTE
MONEY MENTOR
for Women

DEBORAH SMITH PEGUES CPA, MBA

HARVEST HOUSE PUBLISHERS
EUGENE, OREGON

Cover by Kyler Dougherty

Cover photo © vladwel / iStock

Disclaimer

This book is not intended to take the place of sound professional financial, legal, or psychological advice. Neither the author nor the publisher assumes any liability for possible adverse consequences as a result of the information contained herein.

Names and minor details have been changed in the real-life stories shared in this book to protect the privacy of the individuals mentioned.

The One-Minute Money Mentor for Women
Copyright © 2018 Deborah Smith Pegues
Published by Harvest House Publishers
Eugene, Oregon 97408
www.harvesthousepublishers.com

Library of Congress Cataloging-in-Publication Data

Names: Pegues, Deborah Smith, 1950- author.
Title: The one-minute money mentor for women / Deborah Smith Pegues.
Description: Eugene, Or. : Harvest House Publishers, [2018] | Includes
    bibliographical references.
Identifiers: LCCN 2018006865 (print) | LCCN 2018008779 (ebook) | ISBN
    9780736972277 (ebook) | ISBN 9780736972260 (pbk.)
Subjects: LCSH: Wealth--Religious aspects--Christianity. | Finance,
    Personal--Religious aspects--Christianity. | Women--Finance, Personal.
Classification: LCC BR115.W4 (ebook) | LCC BR115.W4 P453 2018 (print) | DDC
    332.0240082--dc23
LC record available at https://lccn.loc.gov/2018006865

Printed in the United States of America

18 19 20 21 22 23 24 25 26 / BP-SK / 10 9 8 7 6 5 4 3 2 1

To my late father,
Rube Smith, Sr.,
who taught me to align my yearnings with my earnings
and to always save for a rainy day.

CONTENTS

PROLOGUE

The Financially Powerless Woman

ell me where you went today or I'm going to blow your brains out!" Robert yelled at his wife. Della cowered on the floor of the bathroom while he held the gun to her head. His rage was fueled by insecurity: He feared Della might someday pay him back by committing adultery as he had done repeatedly during their 20-year marriage.

Fifteen-year-old Sara and her five younger brothers had been awakened by the commotion in the wee hours of the morning. They huddled around the bathroom door and witnessed the traumatizing scene. Robert's verbal and physical abuse was commonplace, but tonight's tirade threatened to have a different outcome.

"Daddy, please don't do it," Sara begged.

As the only girl, she had more clout than the boys and was thus less likely to incur her father's wrath for intervening. Emboldened by her bravery, the boys timidly chimed in with their pleas for mercy.

After what seemed an eternity, Robert finally lowered the gun and crept to bed—totally unaware of the trauma he had inflicted upon his family. This scene would be forever etched in Sara's mind. She loathed her mother's helplessness, her limited education, her lack of money. Della had dropped out of school in the ninth grade, pregnant with their oldest son. Now she could only find work as a part-time house-keeper. Further, she suffered from a chronic foot ailment that often left her unable to walk when her veins became inflamed. She was forced to tolerate Robert's abuse because she depended on him totally for financial support.

Notwithstanding his abusiveness, Robert was a hard worker and a good provider. The neighbors, community, and his church—where he served as a faithful deacon—praised him for the nice house, car, and clothes he provided for his family. The terror that went on behind closed doors was a secret that was not revealed until Della mustered enough courage to flee one day while he was at work.

With the help of a sympathetic niece, Della relocated to the West Coast with six kids in tow and started a new life. She encountered some tough times financially because she had never had the responsibility of providing for the entire household. Nevertheless, they survived with assistance from social welfare, family, friends, and kind neighbors. Della never returned to her abusive situation and never remarried.

Meanwhile, Sara decided in the tiny bathroom that night that she'd never allow herself to be in such a vulnerable position as Della. She vowed to finish high school, work her way through college, land a good job after graduation, and become financially empowered. Any man who attempted to abuse her would be kicked to the curb without a second thought.

Sara did indeed achieve her goals. She became a corporate executive and began to enjoy the good life—with no financial restrictions. She traveled the world, drove a fancy sports car, and dressed fashionably.

But there was just one problem. She was lonely.

The "just try abusing me" chip on her shoulder was so big it discouraged every potential mate who crossed her path. Until she met Jerry. Firm but gentle, God-fearing and understanding, he was just what she needed. They became engaged within a few months after their first date. However, before they tied the knot, he would have to pass a key test.

"I go shopping every Saturday, and I don't plan to stop after we get married," Sara announced one day shortly before the wedding—with a bit of attitude.

"Okay." Jerry shrugged nonchalantly and without further comment. What? Just *okay*? Sara had anticipated a negative response. In fact, for years she had imagined and rehearsed how this conversation would go. Each time she'd heard her father yell at her mother for buying anything besides groceries and household necessities, she'd think, *One day I'm going to have my own money. I won't dare tolerate this kind of madness. I'll shop as much as I like. I can't wait to tell a man that I don't need his money!* Now Jerry, with his unexpected "Okay," had completely thwarted her fantasized fight. All that rehearsing for nothing.

It would take a few more "tests" over the next year for Sara to conclude that Jerry was not going to be like her abusive father. She finally realized it was time to let go of the chip on her shoulder and get ready for a rewarding marriage with good communication and mutual financial goals. Four decades later, she and Jerry are as happy as ever. He handles the household finances and urges her to stop being a penny pincher and to enjoy the fruit of their labor.

While Sara's story has a positive ending, there are still too many women who lack the competence and confidence to become financially empowered. They unwittingly make poor financial decisions, get ripped off, and suffer other detrimental outcomes that they could avoid. I have received e-mails and messages from women of all ages looking for help with their finances. Most have not been abused like Della. In fact, many of them have good, responsible husbands, but the women have surrendered the task of handling household finances to their spouses; thus, they walk in financial darkness, unsure where they stand. I also meet younger and older women who, scarred by the experiences of other women, simply want to become more savvy in handling their money. Still others want to stop being a doormat for their family members.

As women, we cannot expect to experience our best life if we do not have the skills to manage our money—the one tool that King Solomon said "is the answer for everything" (Ecclesiastes 10:19).

But before we get started, let me tell you what the book is *not* about. It's not about rebelling against husbands, reinforcing negative stereotypes some women may have about men and money, or getting rich.

Rather, my goal is to inspire women young and old to acquire the competence and confidence to make informed financial choices that improve the quality of their lives.

Financially speaking, these are the best of times and the worst of times for women. We have more spending power than ever before. We are holding key positions in corporate and political arenas. We have made great inroads into historically male-dominated fields like science, medicine, math, and technology. Women are also the primary providers for the majority of households in the United States.

Although we are exercising strength and performing well in many areas of life, many women are still failing miserably when it comes to handling their finances. Some women have simply resigned themselves to the fact that they just do not "have a head for figures." Others sabotage their financial well-being through a variety of pitfalls that I will address in upcoming chapters. We can do better than this. Hopefully, through the insights and stories of women who have managed their finances well and the lessons learned from those who have not, you will gain the wisdom and understanding you need to achieve financial competence and peace.

I will not limit our discussion to just the mechanics of handling money. Lots of great books and seminars are already available for that. However, I know from years of experience that most financial decisions are driven by emotions and core beliefs. Identifying and forsaking erroneous or limiting beliefs is critical to building a strong financial foundation. So right off the bat, I'll challenge you to examine your core beliefs about money and to make the connection to where you stand today because of them.

My goal is to provide you with a foundational understanding of the financial jargon, concepts, and strategies that will empower you to confidently make informed decisions. You will get the most out of this book if you conclude right now that you have the ability to understand every concept and explanation that I will present. And, that by the grace of God, you will gain the courage to take the next steps to achieve financial peace. Let's get started!

Part 1

FACE YOUR
REALITY

1

EXAMINE YOUR FINANCIAL BELIEFS

Money Mentoring Moment

*Your core beliefs about finances will dictate how you
earn, spend, save, and share your resources.
Your standing today is a reflection of those beliefs.*

When I was growing up, people would often knock on our door, sometimes late into the night, asking my father for a small ($25 to $200) emergency loan. On the surface, he was an unlikely lender. He was not a man of great means, nor did he work at a high-paying job. In fact, as a sawmill foreman, he made just over the minimum wage.

His secret was that he knew how to budget and save his money. He managed well and faithfully provided for a household of nine. He found creative ways to make extra money when bad weather caused the sawmill to be shut down from time to time. He also recognized an opportunity to profit from people whom he described as "those whose yearnings exceeded their earnings." He kept a stash of cash ready for their emergency requests. He didn't lend to everyone who asked, but from those he did, he always required a promissory note with an unusually high interest amount. Note that I said "amount" versus a "rate." You see, he would just state, rather than compute, an amount he felt he should charge. He also required some form of collateral, such as jewelry or the title to a vehicle. The people who failed to repay the loan never got another opportunity to borrow again. He would ultimately sell their collateral, so he did not lose either way. When he died at age 78, he had a large portfolio of outstanding loans. As the executor of his estate, I forgave most of them. I figured the borrowers deserved a break for the exorbitant interest. Notwithstanding, several of them told me that he was a financial refuge for them and many others with poor credit and no other borrowing options.

My mother helped others in a different way. She was very charitable—almost to a fault. She rarely saw a need she didn't try to meet. For instance, the father of a family who lived near us earned a good income—much more than my dad—but the man was financially irresponsible. Therefore, his family always lacked life's necessities. My mother would regularly give our clothes to his kids—without consulting us. One of his daughters and I were in the same class, and we wore the same size. It was not unusual to meet her at school wearing one of my best dresses. Mom said that she just "couldn't stand seeing kids look pitiful like that." Although she didn't have access to much money, she found favor with a couple of retail stores who extended her a charge account. She occasionally allowed friends and relatives to use her credit. She got burned a few times when they failed to pay their charges. I wish I could say that she finally learned her lesson, but she didn't. Even at her death at age 82, several people still owed her money.

Later in life, as I reflected on how my upbringing influenced my financial behavior, I realized that I'd formed several beliefs about money that affected how I managed my own. The most significant belief I held to was that one should never, ever be without a significant cash reserve. Now, there is an upside and a downside to this mind-set. On the upside, it serves as a financial "governor" that causes me to keep debts at bay. On the downside, it has often hindered me from stepping out in faith when I've felt an urging from the Spirit to do so—especially when it would diminish my bank account below my comfort level.

Another one of my strongly held beliefs is that it's best not to make personal loans. However, if you do, you must be very clear about your expectation of being repaid. It is wise to require a signed promissory note lest the borrower assume it's a gift! I find it's just best to prayerfully consider making it a gift from the beginning.

I am a firm believer that all behavior comes out of a belief system. When it comes to finances, our beliefs are the key factor in determining how much money we will earn, spend, save, and share. That's why it's critical that we examine our core beliefs to see which ones work against us and which empower us—but most important, which ones align with the Scriptures and which do not.

Let's look at some common negative beliefs women hold. As we move through each one, I want you to be honest in responding to these three questions:

1. Do I embrace this belief?

2. If so, what effect has it had on my finances, aspirations, or opportunities?

3. How might my life improve if I let go of this belief?

Negative Belief #1: "Wealthy people are materialistic and ungodly."

I only have one question for you if this is your mind-set: Why would God give Abraham, Isaac, Jacob, King Solomon, and many other patriarchs the power to get wealth if having it would make them ungodly? God's reason for granting wealth is revealed in Deuteronomy 8:18: "You shall remember the Lord your God, for it is He who gives you power to get wealth, *that He may establish His covenant*" (NKJV, emphasis added). God's reason for giving wealth is for a specific purpose—to establish His will on earth. Thus, the first question anyone must ask when she acquires wealth is, "Lord, what is Your purpose for these funds?"

When I'm in small, informal social settings and we start to engage in a philosophical discussion, I often like to pose this question: "If you were to come into immediate wealth, what would be your first expenditure?" Depending on their upbringing or spiritual training, most give such answers as, "Pay off my mortgage/debts," "Buy my parents a house/car/other," or "Set aside a majority of the funds for savings." I'm pleasantly surprised when I hear the rare response of, "Pay my tithes (ten percent of income) to my church" or "Donate to a charitable organization." When others respond that buying their dream car or other trappings of success is their top priority, then the "materialistic" label may very well fit them. But keep in mind, that's a choice they make. You have the power to choose differently, to honor God in how you handle the money He entrusts to you.

> **Replacement Belief:** My wealth will enable me to do more and give more to improve the quality of other people's lives.

Negative Belief #2: "If I have abundance, my family and friends might envy me."

How people respond to your abundance will largely be determined by how you handle it. If you brag about it, flaunt it, or demonstrate a superior attitude, they will surely be turned off. However, if you go about doing good (without sounding a horn), keep the subject of your wealth out of your conversations, and behave humbly, you may be surprised at how others will view you.

By the way, why are you anticipating being envied? Could it be that you are projecting your fear onto others because that's how you would respond to a friend's wealth? (Ouch!) If so, you will surely reap what you sow. Maybe it's time to ask God to help you be genuinely happy for others. Applaud them when blessings are manifested in their lives, and do not mention to them another friend who has more blessings than they have. This is a sure sign that you are trying to level the playing field because you may be feeling inferior. Don't let your self-worth decrease just because a friend's net worth increases.

> **Replacement Belief:** God will enable me to handle abundance in a way that inspires others to embrace me and to follow my example.

Negative Belief #3: "I'm afraid money will change who I am."

Money is not a changer of character; it is a revealer. If you are a principled woman before you come into abundance, you can resolve by the grace of God to maintain your standards. Of course, you may have to be more cautious about the kinds of people that abundance can bring into your life, but there is no need to fear that money will hijack your character. Greed, dishonesty, pride, and other financial vices don't leap into our hearts against our will. These negative behaviors often beckon to us based on worldly expectations or desires dormant in our hearts (James 1:14), but we have the power to resist those temptations.

Many years ago (before I got smart and started banking online), I walked into my local branch to make a deposit. I was familiar with the bank manager and a few of the executive employees, so they were aware that my average account balance qualified me for "private banking privileges"—which included not waiting in line. However, on this particular day, I thought I'd forego such entitlements and stand in line with the masses. Maybe I'd even get a chance to work the subject of my faith into a conversation with a stranger.

The wait proved to be unusually long. After a while, I grew impatient. I found myself getting in a huff. *How dare they make me wait!* As I toyed with the idea of closing the account, I realized that I had succumbed to a spirit of pride because they didn't direct me out of the line and into a private office (as was their habit). God hates pride, and we'd better learn to quickly identify and reject it when it manifests in our lives because it is one of the fastest routes to destruction. "Before destruction the heart of a man is haughty, and before honor is humility" (Proverbs 18:12 NKJV).

> **Replacement Belief:** The grace of God empowers me to consistently exercise godly behavior as I manage the resources He entrusts to me.

Negative Belief #4: "If I become wealthy, people will hound me for money."

I hear the fear of saying no in this mind-set. Dear sister, God is not calling us to meet every need that presents itself. That's why we are to acknowledge Him in all our ways so that He may direct our paths (Proverbs 3:5-6). Even if you never become really rich, when people suspect that you have more than enough, they may approach you for financial assistance, but that does not obligate you to always say yes. Of course, many rich people set up foundations or other charities and even hire gatekeepers to manage their charitable activities. While you may not possess the level of resources to warrant such, you may still receive numerous requests for donations—especially once you give any amount to a charity or ministry. One way or another, your name gets out there as a potential donor.

When individuals ask for money, I recommend that you simply get their story—directly or indirectly. Find out if your assistance will help or hurt them in the long run. Then get God's mind on the matter. I've been guilty of enabling and thwarting the spiritual growth of people by not allowing them to reap the consequences of their irresponsible decisions. God may lead you to decline a request because He has a better plan for that person. Or He just may decide to show mercy to the irresponsible person. Let it be His call. Don't let the fear of saying no keep you from embracing the idea of abundance and enjoying God's provisions.

> **Replacement Belief:** I always find great pleasure in helping those in need, and I will also exercise the courage to say no when it is the wise and appropriate response.

Negative Belief #5: "Wealthy people are not happy."

Really? How many wealthy people do you know up close and personal? What is the basis for your judgment? Perhaps you have been influenced by how the media portrays the problems of the rich. Have you ever noticed that wealthy people usually have the same types of issues as regular people—interpersonal conflicts, physical ailments, deaths and tragedies, and emotional fears? Because rich people's wealth gives them a higher public profile, we often attribute their woes to their money. It's not the money; it's called *life*. Numerous studies have been conducted to assess the difference between the life satisfaction level of the rich and poor. The general conclusion is that one group is no happier or sadder than the other.

Don't allow the erroneous assumption that wealthy people are not happy to serve as an excuse not to maximize your financial potential. I should add, however, that wealthy people are often unhappy because they alienate themselves from others and stop enjoying the simpler things of life. The truth of the matter is the key to happiness is meaningful relationships, fulfilling work or hobbies, generous giving, and of course, a close connection to the Almighty.

> **Replacement Belief:** As a wealthy person, I will be as happy as I choose to be. The ball is in my court to stay connected to rewarding relationships and activities and to use my resources for good.

Negative Belief #6: "Poor people have a closer relationship to God."

Well…not always! Job was the richest man in his part of the world. Here is how God described him to Satan: "He is the finest man in all the earth. He is blameless—a man of complete integrity. He fears God and stays away from evil" (Job 1:8 NLT). This rich man had a close relationship to God. Oh, how I would love for God to describe me as "blameless"! It's one thing for others to observe our good character, but when the God of the universe declares someone as blameless, we must take note. Yes, this man Job was rich and righteous. Unlike many rich people, his greatest fear was not that he would lose his wealth. Rather, he feared that his children might offend God at one of their frequent parties at one another's houses. So he faithfully prayed for them that they would not do so (verses 4-5).

What makes us assume that the rich do not seek the heart of God? Did we draw this conclusion based on the tragic story of the rich, young ruler who had kept the Ten Commandments all his life but wanted to know what he must do to inherit eternal life? When Jesus asked him to sell all his possessions, give them to the poor, and follow Him, he sorrowfully declined because he had great riches (Mark 10:17-27). That was his unwise choice. But consider the heart-warming story of Joseph of Arimathea, who requested the body of Jesus after the crucifixion, prepared it for burial, and then placed it in his very own new tomb. Matthew 27:57 simply states that he was "rich" and that he was "a disciple of Jesus." I'm thrilled that this rich man had chosen to follow Jesus. He was financially positioned to give our Savior a proper burial.

Now, regarding poor people, they do indeed have more motivation to pray to God, because without adequate financial resources for food, shelter, medical assistance, and other essentials, God is their only hope. Who better to ask for help than the One who owns it all? But not every poor person seeks His provision. Some resort to theft, violence, and other negative actions to survive. The truth of the matter is that rich and poor can be as close to God as they choose to be; money is not the deciding factor.

> **Replacement Belief:** My intimacy with God is not determined by the level of my resources. I can be as close to God as I choose to be.

Negative Belief #7: "The cards are stacked against me."

When struggling financially, it's tempting to believe that gender, ethnicity, looks, or other factors are keeping you down. But Scripture speaks directly to that belief through one of the most empowering and comforting passages in the Bible: "The LORD Almighty has purposed, and who can thwart him? His hand is stretched out, and who can turn it back?" (Isaiah 14:27).

I have cemented this truth into my heart and have had to remind myself of it countless times during my professional career. Like the time when I worked as a VP of a major corporation and my male officemates were bent on sabotaging my career with their dirty politics. I clung to the truth that absolutely no one—*no one*—could thwart God's plans for me. And indeed, God foiled their every attempt.

Ladies, let this truth infiltrate your heart and mind to the point where you can ignore someone's attempt to disadvantage you in any way. If you don't get beyond this erroneous belief, you will always blame somebody else for your financial plight. Or you will be convinced that your success is dependent upon your connections to the right people.

Only two women have books of the Bible named after them—Esther and Ruth. They were both foreigners in the land where they made history and fulfilled their purpose in financial comfort. Esther hid her Jewish identity and won the beauty contest to become the next queen of Persia after Vashti, the original queen, was dethroned for refusing the king's command to parade herself before his drunken guests. Later, Haman, a top-ranking Persian official, decided to destroy the entire Jewish population because Mordecai, Esther's cousin, wouldn't bow to him. Queen Esther appealed to her husband, the king, revealed her heritage, and saved the Jewish people from annihilation. (Read the entire book of Esther for the details of this exciting story.)

Ruth was from the land of Moab. She remained loyal to her Jewish mother-in-law, Naomi, after Ruth's husband died. Rather than returning to her people, she committed to supporting Naomi by working in the fields in Jerusalem. However, God gave her favor with Boaz, a wealthy cousin of her deceased husband. He married her according to the law and redeemed her—and Naomi—from a life of poverty. Ruth became the great-grandmother of King David, which landed her in the lineage of Jesus.

The stories of these two women demonstrate that God's purpose and plan for our lives cannot be derailed by any negative circumstances.

> **Replacement Belief:** God has determined my destiny, and no one can thwart it based on my gender, ethnicity, or any other factor.

These are just a sampling of the beliefs and assumptions that will derail your finances. Let's renounce them all right now with this simple prayer: *"Father, by Your grace I reject every erroneous or limiting belief that threatens to sabotage my finances. I ask that You open the eyes of my understanding and cause me to embrace the truths that will set me free to soar financially. In the name of Jesus, I pray. Amen."*

2

DETERMINE WHERE YOU STAND

Money Mentoring Moment

Knowing where you are is always critical to getting where you want to go. You must courageously face the reality of your existing assets, debts, income, and spending levels before you can develop a strategy for changing your financial situation.

There is nothing better than a good dose of reality to motivate you to action. Yes, it can be scary and depressing to come face-to-face with overwhelming financial obligations and the glaring lack of income to meet them, but ignoring them will only make matters worse.

Meet Sherry. She had been a pampered princess most of her married life—until her husband contracted a terminal illness and passed away. He had tried to give her a heads-up on the various financial issues she and their two minor children would face, but she had refused to engage in any conversations about his imminent death. When the fateful day came, she was devastated by the loss of her loving companion and loyal security blanket. She had little insight into the cost of running their household and the business he owned. Further, she had convinced herself that since she was a creative person she did not have a "head for figures." She spent several months in denial—depressed, dodging creditors, and refusing to open the unending stack of bills that arrived daily.

Finally, she called her friend Joan over to help her find her way out of the mire. Joan led her through the following exercise that all women would be wise to complete or review on a regular basis. You see, it was during the process of organizing Sherry's bills to see where she stood that she and her friend Joan discovered a huge royalty check (in the stack of unopened mail) from a recording company for whom Sherry had written a hit song several years earlier. The amount was enough to make a significant impact on her outstanding bills.

Getting the Scoop on Where You Stand

Much like the sign at the entrance of the shopping mall that says, "You are here," you must first determine where you are financially. Trust me, knowing where you stand will result in a lot less anxiety than putting your head in the sand. I'm going to warn you now that the rest of this chapter may sound like a crash course in accounting. Fear not, I taught beginning accounting at a major university for over ten years. For most of the students, English was not their first language, so I prayed often for ways to make the concepts easy to grasp. By the end of this chapter you will know how to prepare and interpret two essential financial statements that determine where you stand and where your money is going.

The first statement, the Balance Sheet—also known as a Statement of Financial Position—is a snapshot of what you own (assets) and what you owe (liabilities) at a specific point in time. The difference between total assets and total liabilities is called *net worth* on a personal Balance Sheet and *net equity* for a business. The Balance Sheet does not reveal what you make or what you spend; it simply shows where you *stand* on a given date.

To understand how to prepare and interpret this statement, let's take a look at the Balance Sheet of "Sarah Jones" and see where she stands.

When preparing your Balance Sheet, first list your assets in the order of *liquidity*, that is, how quickly you can convert them into cash. Obviously, cash is the most liquid of all assets.

	Sarah Jones		
	Balance Sheet*		
	As of December 31, 20XX		
	ASSETS (what she owns)		
			(Market Value)*
1	Checking/Savings	$	1,500
2	Accounts Receivable		2,000
3	Cash Value—Whole Life Insurance Policy		2,000
4	Vehicle		24,500
5	Home		200,000
6	Jewelry, Clothes		5,000
7	Retirement Plan/Investments		9,000
8	Other Assets		1,000
9	TOTAL ASSETS	$	245,000
	LIABILITIES (what she owes)		
10	Credit Cards/Revolving Credit		13,000
11	Auto Loan		20,000
12	Mortgage		150,000
13	**TOTAL** LIABILITIES		183,000
14	NET WORTH (ASSETS (9) minus LIABILITIES (13))		62,000
15	TOTAL LIABILITIES & NET WORTH	$	245,000

For a Personal Balance Sheet, the Assets will be shown at Fair Market Value (FMV); however, businesses must use "historical cost," i.e., the cost of the item minus all depreciation taken on it since it was obtained.

Let's now take a deeper look at where Sarah stands by reviewing each line item. I suggest you say each numbered line item out loud (okay, say it in your head if you are reading in a public place). I want you to get used to understanding what items are included on this vital statement. Lines 1 through 9 list the various categories of Assets; Lines 10-13 disclose the categories of liabilities.

Line 1—*Checking/Savings:* Sarah has only $1,500 in cash. Actually, this is more than the average cash balance held by the typical American adult, according to a 2016 survey by GOBankingRates.com. The countrywide survey of over 7,000 respondents revealed that 69 percent of Americans have under $1,000 in savings; 34 percent had zero savings.[1] Where is Sarah's reserve for unexpected car repairs, medical bills, a job layoff/shutdown, or other emergencies? Glaringly absent.

Line 2—*Accounts Receivable:* This is the amount due from others such as temporary personal loans to family or friends or payments from clients or customers that Sarah has done independent work for. *Receivable* simply means "able to receive." Thus, it is important that Sarah only includes here the amount that she can reasonably expect to receive. If the amount has been outstanding more than a year, it's time for her to get real about whether it is really collectable. If there is no possibility of collection, the amount due is not an asset. Thus, it should not be included as it has no value.

Line 3—*Cash Value—Whole Life Insurance Policy:* When one purchases *whole life* or universal insurance coverage (versus *term* life insurance), a portion of the premiums is invested and the policy builds up a cash value that you may cash out or borrow against. This type of insurance is usually not as good a deal as agents make it out to be. However, the cash value is still an asset. See chapter 20 for a more detailed discussion.

Line 4—*Vehicle:* This is the estimated value of Sarah's car, truck, or other vehicle. (You may find the average price your vehicle is going for in your area at the Kelley Blue Book site at *www.kbb.com.*)

Line 5—*Home:* This is the estimated fair market value (FMV) of Sarah's house or condo. No need to invest in an official appraisal for this exercise. Simply obtain a ballpark figure for a home by entering the address at such sites as *www.zillow.com* or *www.realtor.com.*

Line 6—*Jewelry, Clothes, Etc.:* Use approximate values here. I pray that this is not the most significant dollar amount on any woman's Balance Sheet.

Line 7—*Retirement Plan/Investments:* This amount represents the current value of the portfolio based on the most recent statement from the plan manager of the 401(k), 403(b), or other retirement funds.

Line 8—*Other Assets:* This includes everything else Sarah owns that has value (stamp or coin collections, artwork, etc.).

Line 9—With $245,000 in *Total Assets,* one might assume Sarah is doing okay. However, we cannot draw a conclusion about where she stands without analyzing and understanding the claims against those assets. That's what the *Liabilities* section of the Balance Sheet will reveal.

Line 10—*Credit Cards/Revolving Credit:* Oh no! Sarah has $13,000 in credit card debt. From the list of her assets, it doesn't appear that she purchased investments with her credit cards. Nope, looks like whatever she bought was totally consumed. Maybe too many social outings? Lavish vacations? Medical bills? We will suspend judgment and just observe that Sarah is not in a strong financial position with only $1,500 in cash and such a high level of credit card debt.

Line 11—*Auto Loan:* Sarah owes $20,000 on the $24,500 vehicle listed on Line 4. Well, $4,500 equity in her car is better than no equity. I just wish she could have paid cash for it or at least made a larger down payment. Because cars depreciate so quickly, she just may find that in a year or so, she owes more on the car than it's worth.

Line 12—*Mortgage:* Sarah obviously had good enough credit at some point in the past to qualify for a $150,000 mortgage to purchase her home now valued at $200,000. With lenders' strict qualifying standards, we can safely assume that most of Sarah's credit card debt was incurred after she purchased the house. Perhaps moving costs, repairs, or improvements were the culprits. Even so, we must applaud her for making the investment, for she now has $50,000 in home equity.

Line 13—Sarah has $183,000 in *Total Liabilities* or "claims" against her $245,000 in *Total Assets.* Now it's time to compute her *Net Worth.*

Line 14—*Net Worth* is simply the difference between Total Assets and Total Liabilities. If Sarah were to sell everything she owns and pay off all her debts, she would have $62,000 left. This is her Net Worth. Certainly not enough to retire on, but better than nothing.

Unfortunately, many women have a negative net worth; their liabilities exceed their assets. Therefore, even if they were to sell everything, they could not pay off all their debts. They would still be in the red. If this is your plight, don't despair. Your situation will improve as you become more savvy and intentional about your financial plan.

Line 15—The official Balance Sheet formula is *Total Assets = Total Liabilities + Net Worth.* It is merely a computation to determine the Net Worth or Net Equity of the owner of the Balance Sheet.

I cannot stress enough the importance of this exercise in letting you know where you stand. However, we are not finished yet. You must also get a good handle on what you earn or receive and where it goes. It's time to prepare a Statement of Cash Receipts and Disbursements. Unlike the Balance Sheet, which is a snapshot of where you stand at a certain *point* in time, this statement will disclose how much you received and spent over a certain *period* of time. Usually the period is for a month, quarter, or year. Monthly is the traditional period used for budgeting, so let's see what level of cash flow Sarah is experiencing.

	Sarah Jones		
	Statement of Cash Receipts & Disbursements		
	(What She Earns and Where It Goes)		
1	Income (Take-home from all sources)	$	4,000
2	Less: Charitable Contributions		(400)
3	Less: Savings (5% minimum)		(200)
4	**Cash Available**		**3,400**
5	Less: Fixed Expenditures (Rent/Mortgage, Insurance, Car Note, Credit Card Minimum Payment, Utilities, etc.)		(2,500)
6	Less: Discretionary Expenditures (Lunches/Dinners, Groceries, Grooming, Phones, Entertainment/Recreation, etc.)		(800)
7	Total Fixed & Discretionary Expenditures		(3,300)
8	**Excess Cash Available**	$	**100**

This Statement of Cash Receipts and Disbursements is pretty self-explanatory.

Line 1—*Income:* Sarah is bringing home $4,000 a month from her $5,200 gross pay. The company deducts the required Social Security and income tax withholdings, and voluntary deductions.

Line 2—*Charitable Contributions:* If you are not a tither, then you are probably questioning the wisdom of Sarah paying ten percent of her income to her church. Sarah believes that according to Matthew 23:23 (NLT), tithing is important. "What sorrow awaits you teachers of religious law and you Pharisees. Hypocrites! For you are careful to tithe even the tiniest income from your herb gardens, but you ignore the more important aspects of the law—justice, mercy, and faith. You should tithe, yes, but do not neglect the more important things." The Pharisees had unwisely elevated tithing as the supreme act of piety, but Jesus reminded them that there were other actions and behaviors that were even more important. However, if Jesus says we *should* do something, then indeed we should. Thus, I agree with Sarah's decision to tithe. At the time of this writing, my husband and I have been faithful tithers for almost 39 years. And while we have experienced layoffs and other economic downturns, we have never lacked, lost, or longed for anything. We attribute our good fortune to the grace of God and our obedience to His command to put Him first in our finances. I'm not dogmatic about whether you tithe or not; therefore, I don't judge you one way or the other. I'm just sharing our testimony. Feel free to be fully persuaded in your own mind. We certainly are!

Line 3—*Savings:* Rather than saving only five percent of her pay, I'd like to see Sarah get that number up to at least ten percent so that she may more quickly reach a minimum $3,300 emergency reserve, i.e., the equivalent of one month's living expenses (per Line 7). She would also position herself for a better retirement. She currently has her employer deducting only one percent of her paycheck for the company's retirement plan even though they offer three percent matching. She's not grasping the fact that she is leaving free money on the table each pay period.

Line 4—*Cash Available* is the amount Sarah has available to cover her Fixed and Discretionary living expenses.

Lines 5-7—*Expenditures:* Sarah would be wise to review each expenditure category and decide which ones she can reduce or eliminate to achieve her savings and other goals. She should not approach the task as a dreaded exercise but as a tool help her gain control of her finances.

Line 8—*Excess Cash Available:* Sarah has $100 each month in excess cash flow. What should she do with these funds? We will look more closely at how to prioritize expenditures in the next chapter. For now, Sarah has achieved a major milestone; she has determined where she stands. Mission accomplished.

By the way, now that we have worked through the two essential statements and you can clearly see that you can prepare these manually (you can also create your own forms using the spreadsheets in the appendices on pages 209 and 211), you've probably already guessed there are some wonderful, user-friendly software programs available such as Quicken (*Quicken.com*) and YNAB (*youneedabudget.com*) that will eliminate the need for spreadsheets or manual forms. You will be on the road to financial empowerment when you easily enter your financial transactions, instantly see your spending history and how you are faring with respect to your budget, project your cash flow, and much more. Don't be intimidated by the notion of using such software. Embrace it; it can only make you more informed and more financially powerful. Most of all, keep the faith, ladies! Always expect God to show Himself strong in your circumstances.

3

ESTABLISH WISE FINANCIAL PRIORITIES

Money Mentoring Moment

*A key factor in gaining control over your finances
is to know what priorities to pursue based on
your unique situation; such a strategy requires
counsel, commitment, and consistency.*

Setting goals is one of the most empowering acts you can perform to secure your financial future. You may have heard the saying, "Aim at nothing and you will hit it every time." Setting goals means knowing where you want to go and having a plan for getting there. Jesus Himself talked about setting goals. In Luke 14:28-32, He stresses the importance of planning—whether you are building a tower or going to war. His core message was "analyze the cost." Assess the adequacy of your resources. It is prudent to count the cost to ensure you have the resources and motivation necessary; otherwise, failure is imminent.

The benefits of goal setting are numerous and include the following:

- Aiding in day-to-day spending decisions. Before making even small purchases, it is smart to evaluate whether a proposed expenditure will help move you closer to or away from your goals.

- Providing motivation. There's a difference between saving just because you know you should and saving toward specific goals such as the down payment on a house, a major purchase, or a wealth-building objective. Goal-oriented decisions are a greater motivator because you will receive a reward in the end.

- Curtailing procrastination. Procrastination, the opposite of motivation, often hinders financial goals. If your goal is to increase your credit score, you will think twice before being late on a bill. If you need to save for your next semester of college, you aren't likely to delay putting the money aside.

- Increasing confidence. In all areas of life, making better decisions and taking steps to reach your goals results in feeling better about yourself, which further enhances your desire to make good decisions.

- Developing consistency. Goals help ensure that your plans match your behavior. When you have a goal in the forefront of your mind, it is difficult to act in opposition to it.

In order to plan your path to financial peace, it's important to divide goals into short- and long-term. This will help avoid frustration and impatience when some goals take a bit longer. Short-term goals generally take less than two years to complete, while long-term goals take two years or longer.

Examples of Short-Term Goals:

- Saving your first $1,000 for an emergency fund
- Paying off a small debt, such as a medical bill or a credit card with a low balance

Examples of Long-Term Goals:

- Saving a $10,000 down payment to purchase a house
- Paying off student loan debt
- Investing for retirement

Prioritizing Your Financial Goals

It's one thing to establish goals, but the real challenge is to determine which ones to pursue first. Here is a prioritized list to facilitate the process:

1. Reaffirm your financial goals. Own them. Once you commit to them, you can implement a strategy.

2. As an act of faith and obedience, tithe ten percent of your income to the place where you are spiritually fed.

3. Establish a specific plan to lower or eliminate debt. You can download a debt payoff app such as Debt Free or Debt Payoff Pro straight to your phone or tablet. These apps are simple to use and let you see the impact of a plan before you implement it. This can be very motivating when you are tempted to abandon it.

4. Perform a regular financial checkup on all aspects of your plan. As you work through it, do periodic assessments to determine where you stand and whether you need to make any adjustments to reach your goals.

5. Save at least ten percent of your earnings if possible. If this is not feasible right away, it would be wise to start at whatever level you can and increase the amount as you are able. Don't just save "more" but target a specific amount by a set date. Savings prevent you from going into debt when the inevitable emergencies arise. If your employer has a savings program, take advantage of it.

Planning Versus Living by Faith

In Matthew 6:25-34, Jesus taught the proper mind-set regarding the daily needs of life, such as food and clothing. He concludes His message in verse 34: "Don't worry about tomorrow, for tomorrow will bring its own worries. Today's trouble is enough for today" (NLT). Some Christians find this confusing and often wonder, "Is there a way to reconcile planning and the Lord's command to live by faith?"

Yes, most certainly. When Jesus said, "Don't worry," He didn't mean "don't think about" or "don't plan"—He simply meant "don't worry." The idea is not to be anxious about things you can't control because God has promised to take care of our daily needs. But that doesn't negate the need for planning. For our part, we should do everything within our power and then recognize what is outside our control and leave it up to God. Pray and plan, but don't fret. God "will supply every need of yours according to his riches in glory in Christ Jesus" (Philippians 4:19 ESV).

Consider the story of the ten virgins in Matthew 25:1-13. They went out to meet the bridegroom, all carrying lamps. Five virgins had the foresight to bring along extra oil and five did not. Eventually they all fell asleep waiting for the bridegroom. At midnight, when the message rang out that he was nearby, the five "foolish" virgins found that their lamps were extinguishing, so they asked the "wise" virgins to share their oil. The wise virgins refused. "But the wise answered, saying, 'No, lest there should not be enough for us and you; but go rather to those who sell, and buy for yourselves,'" (Matthew 25:9 NKJV). So the foolish virgins left to go purchase some, but by the time they returned, the bridegroom had arrived and taken the wise virgins in with him to the wedding banquet. When the foolish virgins tried to enter, it was too late. The door was shut tight. They could have easily avoided this problem. Lack of funds was not the issue—as evidenced by the fact that they went to buy more. So even though they had money to buy extra oil, they didn't plan ahead to ensure their oil didn't run out.

Seeking Counsel

What do you do if your finances are in such bad shape that you can't even begin to figure out what goals you should set? There's no shame in getting help. As Proverbs 12:15 reminds us, "The wise listen to advice."

Credit counseling agencies can provide help in a variety of ways. Depending on your income, some may even offer their services for free or at a low cost. In addition to helping you get a handle on your finances by reducing or eliminating debt, some also offer financial education. We will discuss credit counseling services in more depth in chapter 5, "Master Your Debts."

Finding Creative Solutions

Sometimes setting goals isn't as easy as just writing them down and making a plan. There are times when more creativity is required. Perhaps you don't yet have the resources you need or you face a unique set of circumstances. Whatever the problem, creative solutions can help provide the motivation to get started and the momentum to keep going. Goals often seem doable when they are merely ideas. Then they fall apart when implementation begins. Here are some ideas to stimulate your creative juices.

Create a vision board. If a written list isn't doing the trick, perhaps your mind needs more stimulation. A vision board can provide that. The concept is simple. Use poster board, chalkboard, white board, or even the wall as a starting point to brainstorm ideas. Then review magazines, newspapers, Internet photos, and books to find pictures that help you visualize your goals. Tape or glue these items to your canvas in whatever order seems best until you have a good picture of where you want to go and how you might get there. You can even draw images and write text on your board; there's no right or wrong way to do it. In this digital age, you can even create one or more Pinterest (*pinterest .com*) boards to accomplish the same thing.

Think outside the box. If you are trying to reach a goal that seems impossible because of where you are in your life, consider alternative paths that will allow you to move in the direction of your goals. For example, perhaps you want to produce movies, but you are deep in debt, can't afford any equipment, and have limited knowledge and experience regarding the industry. Instead of focusing on the millions you think you need to get started, begin thinking about the little things you can do right now. Watch YouTube videos about making movies. Take an inexpensive introductory class on the subject. Make friends with someone majoring in cinema and volunteer to shadow that person around as her "Girl Friday" as he or she films. Arrange to visit the set of a Hollywood movie in the making. Every step you take, however small, moves you one step closer to your ultimate goal. Don't let obstacles hinder you; rather, use them as stepping-stones. Doing the one thing you can do now just may open the door to the next thing.

Join a goal-setting community. Humans are simply better together. Everything is more fun and easier when you can share it with others. Many people have joined forces online to keep each other accountable for their goals. Various websites and apps now make it extremely easy to keep track of your goals and share your progress. Some sites even make it more interesting by assessing a monetary penalty if you don't reach your goals. In addition, seeing other people consistently meet their goals can encourage you to keep trying. When you get discouraged, and even if you temporarily fail, such communities can act as a cheerleading squad to help you get back on track. Try an app such as *joesgoals.com* or *lifetick.com* to get started, or simply Google "goal setting sites" to find one that fits you.

Stay Balanced

Listen, ladies, do not go to the extreme in trying to reach your financial goals. I know I'm going against the teaching of several popular financial gurus in telling you not to give up your lattes until you have six months of living expenses in the bank. I'm certainly not saying to splurge on luxuries every day; however, you can enjoy a treat without waiting forever to do so. Just include it on your prioritized plan and offset it against another category of expenditures.

You can do this. Embrace your goal with enthusiasm and good intentions, and before you know it you will arrive at your desired financial destination empowered and with great experience and wisdom to share with others.

4

GET FINANCIALLY INTIMATE BEFORE AND AFTER YOU SAY "I DO"

Money Mentoring Moment

You and your mate must get financially naked and agree on common goals in order to achieve true intimacy and an economically stable relationship.

My marriage to my husband, Darnell, has been fairly smooth sailing—even though we tied the knot on April 14, the anniversary of the *Titanic* striking an iceberg! However, from time to time we have navigated some choppy waters because of our different philosophies about money. Realizing that our financial mind-sets are a reflection of our upbringing and other life experiences, we've worked hard to understand ourselves and each other in our quest for financial harmony.

Though we do not claim to have totally mastered the challenge, we have aligned our financial priorities with each other's—and God's—and gotten on the path to financial intimacy. We define *financial intimacy* as "the state in a couple's relationship in which each can openly, honestly, and safely express their financial beliefs, fears, and expectations and know that their partner will listen and respond without judgment or ridicule."

Interestingly, as a certified public accountant and life coach, I've observed that most financial conflicts in marriages are not caused by a *lack* of money but rather a couple's failure to agree on financial *priorities*. Thus, learning how to come to mutual agreement on financial issues is critical to a high-quality marriage. In the words of the Old Testament prophet Amos, "Can two people walk together without agreeing on the direction?" (Amos 3:3 NLT).

Financial Intimacy Before Marriage

Almost every couple contemplating marriage tends to avoid or gloss over the dreaded "financial talk." Well, it may not be romantic, but it is certainly revealing when you get insight into your future husband's financial beliefs, habits, and history. My heart's desire is to see couples approach this crucial exercise with ease and an intent to understand. Therefore, I developed the 20-question quiz below to facilitate the conversation and to reveal areas of potential conflict. Rather than sucking the romance out of the relationship, completing this exercise just may be the key to keeping your marriage on solid ground as you go into it with your financial eyes wide open about your man's money mind-set (as well as your own) and potential money pitfalls.

A Premarital 20/20 Vision Quiz for Financial Compatibility[1]

Instructions: The purpose of this quiz is to determine if a couple has the same vision for their finances. Each party must honestly answer "T" for true or "F" for false to each of the questions below. When finished, they should compare their answers and candidly discuss areas for potential conflict. A "true" answer to any of the questions by either party should be considered a red flag that should not be ignored.

	HIM	HER	
1			I do not give to the church or other charities.
2			I do not systematically save money out of my income.
3			I have less than four weeks' take-home pay in reserve.

	HIM	HER	
4			I do not maintain a bank account; I prefer to pay my bills by cash or money order.
5			I have no dream of purchasing a home.
6			I buy status symbols (cars/clothes, etc.) that fit the image I wish to portray to others.
7			I do not believe that a wife should work outside the home.
8			I believe that whoever makes the most money should have the final say in making household financial decisions.
9			I believe that all bills should be split 50-50.
10			I feel that there is nothing wrong with a spouse having a "secret" bank account as long as she or he pays her or his share of the bills.
11			I do not participate in my employer's matching contribution retirement program. Or if self-employed: I do not make any contributions toward my retirement.
12			I have had at least three different employers in the past five years.
13			I often pick up the tab when I eat out with family and friends—even if I have to charge the bill because I am short on cash.
14			My FICO score is under 675.
15			I see no problem in co-signing for or extending a personal loan to a close friend or family member.
16			I am only able to make the minimum payment on my credit cards and other consumer debt.
17			I am currently delinquent on a personal or other debt.
18			I have filed for bankruptcy in the past ten years.
19			I have a financial commitment to a former spouse, parent, child, business partner, or other that will continue after I am married.
20			I feel that it is okay to tell a "little white lie" to save money or to gain other financial advantage.

If you choose to ignore this exam, thinking that "love will cover all," wake up! When you wed, you are marrying your mate's financial history. Your ability to buy a house, to obtain favorable credit terms, and other financial considerations are at stake. Start out on a foundation of truth and full disclosure, and you will lower the risk of experiencing one of the top causes of divorce—financial conflict.

Financial Intimacy After the Vows

Maybe you are already married and somehow the "financial talk" never happened before you said, "I do." Such was the case with Sharon.

> I know nothing about my husband Jack's finances after being married for more than two years. Our pastor suggested we have a "financial talk" before marriage, but Jack kept wiggling out of it. For the most part, we handle our bills separately. He pays for almost everything. I pay for my car, the family cell phones, and my personal bills. Jack is the sweetest husband and will do anything for me—except talk finances. He wants us to have a baby next year; however, I don't feel comfortable having a child if we aren't fully integrated as a couple financially. What should I do?

Perhaps your mate, like Jack, may be uncomfortable having "the talk." Don't despair; it's not too late. Here's how you can open a safe door for the dreaded discussion. Try formulating a nonthreatening, non-accusatory request to put the conversation in motion.

> "Jack, I'd love to know the attitudes and experiences that shaped your financial personality and mind-set. I promise not to judge or critically evaluate what you share with me. I'm just seeking to understand. I'm willing to share mine first, if you'd like."

Now proceed to the questions below. Don't rush through them. Listen to his responses and ask follow-up questions if you feel clarity is needed. Seek to understand. Be empathetic. Don't interrupt. You can even choose to keep the discussion lighthearted to take the edge off. My husband and I had a great time doing this several years into our marriage and felt much closer when we finished.

- "When you were growing up, was money a source of tension, fights, or stress in your family?"

- "Who controlled the money or exerted the most power over how it was spent? Did you feel it was fair or unfair? Why?"

- "Did you have all your basic needs met (shelter, food, clothing, etc.)? If not, what resolve or vow, if any, did you make back then to make sure your experience would be different in the future?"

After you have waded into these deep waters, now is the time to address other essential issues:

- Agree on your top financial priorities:
  - » when and if you will purchase a home, what size, the "must haves" to be included
  - » the desired level of your emergency cash reserve
  - » if your paychecks will be combined or separated
  - » who will be responsible for paying bills and handling other household finances

- Confirm the named beneficiaries on his life insurance policies. Otherwise, you may end up like Monique. Her husband, Jim, battled cancer for eight years. When he passed away, she learned that he had failed to name her as the new beneficiary when they got married. Rather, his sister was listed. Monique was livid and without adequate funds to bury him. The sister felt no responsibility to share the proceeds with the cash-strapped, grieving wife. This is also a good time to confirm the beneficiaries on your life insurance policies.

- Confirm the authorized signers (and beneficiaries) for all bank accounts and make sure both your names are on the accounts.

- Record and store in a safe place the online passwords for all bank, investments, credit card accounts, and insurance policies. Keep this information in a handy but secure place. Be sure to update and share your records each time you change them!

- If he had a prior marriage, review the divorce decree to confirm the official date of the divorce. Sally unwisely lived with her fiancé Bill for several years. When he passed away suddenly, his former wife successfully claimed his insurance proceeds. Bill had never finalized the divorce. Sally was left in dire straits with their two children.

- Stay in the know. You may have married the most financially responsible man on the planet, but you must still stay in the know on the status of your assets, liabilities, and other aspects of your finances. Do not relegate this responsibility totally to your husband. You never know when he will make his transition to eternity and you will have to assume responsibility for managing your own resources. Take some time periodically and review the bank statements, checkbook, debit card records, etc. Know where the insurance policies are stored and how to contact the company. No nodding on this one!

Unspoken Rules for When You Make the Most Money

Because women have made significant advances in the workplace, in many cases they earn more than their husbands. Depending on his level of confidence or emotional security, this could be problematic. Here are some critical reminders if this is your situation:

- Do not feel that you need to periodically remind him of the gap between your incomes; it's already a known reality.

- Never use your superior earnings as justification for attempting to control your husband or lord them over him. Remember that you are in a covenant relationship and the two of you have become one. Ideally, everything that comes into the household belongs to the marriage. The sooner you adopt this mind-set, the happier you will be.

- Never use his meager earnings history to belittle him no matter how frustrated you get. Remember that words never die. They could create a wound that will fester and cause deep resentment for the rest of your marriage. One rising celebrity declared on national television that her husband of more than 25 years "had no money." He could not get beyond the humiliation. They divorced shortly thereafter.

- If you feel your husband has gotten a bit too comfortable with you being the main breadwinner, clarify your expectations—with wisdom: "John, it looks like your motivation to find better employment has waned. You are a talented, smart man, and I believe there is a better job or money-making opportunity just waiting for you. I know you want to maximize your contribution to our living expenses. Let's pray and believe God for an open door for you to generate more income. How can I help you? We are in this together."

Dealing with a Financially Irresponsible Husband

If your man demonstrates irresponsible financial behavior, discuss it with him the minute it rears its head. If you go silent, it could only make things worse as silence implies consent. Calmly sit down and establish or reconfirm your financial goals.

"Are we still on the same page regarding what we are trying to achieve (an emergency reserve of X amount, paying off credit cards, etc.)? Let's review our plan for getting there." Here is the script that one of my wise pastor friends advised: "Your current habits are not helping our progress. I need your support."

Seek God's direction regarding what actions to take to protect the well-being of the household. The story of Abigail in 1 Samuel 25 provides a good model. Before David became the new king of Israel, he was forced to go on the run from the insecure King Saul who felt David threatened his kingdom. David and his troops hid out in the hills. At one point their presence served as a wall of protection from potential raiders for the flock of a certain rich landowner named Nabal. Once, when their food supply ran low, David sent a delegation to Nabal's home to ask for provisions. Surely he would want to reciprocate the kindness they had extended to his workers.

The surly tycoon refused to help them and hurled insults at them. David was so ticked off when his men told him about Nabal's response that he ordered them to suit up to go and kill every man in Nabal's household. How dare he! Fortunately, one of Nabal's servants had witnessed the dialogue with the delegation and warned Nabal's wife, Abigail, that there might be trouble because of how Nabal had treated David's soldiers. She quickly put together an impressive bundle of food items for the army and headed out behind the servants who were to deliver them. "She said to her servants, 'Go on before me; see, I am coming after you.' But she did not tell her husband Nabal" (1 Samuel 25:19 NKJV). Sometimes a woman's gotta do what she's gotta do when the well-being of the household is at stake.

Abigail met David and his men en route to her home. Her passionate plea for him not to retaliate against her foolish husband is one for the record books. "When the Lord has done all he promised and has made you leader of Israel, don't let this be a blemish on your record. Then your conscience won't have to bear the staggering burden of needless bloodshed and vengeance" (1 Samuel 25:30-31 NLT). Her words quelled his anger. Because of her decisive actions, a tragedy was averted. Later, when Nabal sobered up, she told him all that had happened. He had a heart attack and died several days later. Hearing the news of Nabal's death, David sent for Abigail to become his wife.

Listen, ladies, if your husband's behavior is jeopardizing the well-being of the household, you may have to take steps to protect or temporarily redirect the family resources. You may have to remove his access to household funds until he goes through counseling and learns to become more financially responsible. Boundaries are critical here, and all boundary violations must have consequences in order to be effective. I know this may sound mean, controlling, or generally negative to some of you who can't stand the thought of possible abandonment, so please connect with a good support system of people who can encourage you to be strong in insisting on a change in behavior. Stay on your path to financial empowerment.

6 Secrets of a Caring Confrontation: The Key to Building a Stable Marriage

Whether in football, basketball, or any other team sport, it's essential that players on the same team communicate with one another in order to run their plays. If you and your mate are experiencing financial turmoil, talk about it. Burying your head in the sand will most likely put you on a collision course with divorce. Your marriage does not have to become a statistic. You can overcome financial tension or thwart its development with a caring confrontation. Yes, confrontation. Sounds hostile? Not when you do it God's way. I encourage you to commit now to confronting and resolving those thorny financial and relational issues that threaten your unity. Here are six surefire strategies for an effective confrontation.

1. Select the right time and place to put the issue on the table; don't be guilty of doing the right thing at the wrong time! Don't try to force your mate to communicate when he is tired, hungry, distracted, or stressed.

2. Be specific about the behavior you find problematic. Yes, use the Sandwich Approach; begin and end with a positive statement or affirmation (bread), but for goodness' sake, don't generalize or beat around the bush so much that your spouse loses sight of the specific problem (meat).

3. Seek first to understand his rationale. Don't accuse. Simply listen, listen, listen.

4. Make constructive comments only. Do not attack your mate's character or judgment. Just stay focused on the behavior that needs to change.

5. Agree on future behavior. Develop and commit to specific guidelines or strategies for going forward. This is also a good time to agree on the consequences when the boundaries are violated.

6. Always, always speak of your possessions (including houses, cars, and even your children and stepchildren) as "ours" rather than "my" or "mine." If you're going to walk in unity with your husband, you must practice unity talk!

Of course, if you are the one who needs to be confronted, then your husband would use this same approach to guide the conversation. Don't resist it; embrace it.

5

MASTER YOUR DEBTS

Money Mentoring Moment

*Debt is a burden that we should seek to minimize
or eliminate. We must understand the difference
between good debt and bad debt and always
walk in integrity when dealing with creditors.*

In almost every area of life, the world has a different standard of living than God does. The area of finances is no different. Borrowing is a natural part of our lives. Each year billions are wasted on interest payments, annual fees, and late fees. The key to changing bad habits is to start with changing your mind-set. Our society has demonstrated that debt is the American way, but common practice isn't always common sense. Let's review God's view of debt:

- Being debt-free is considered a blessing. "If you fully obey the LORD your God and carefully follow all his commands I give you today, the LORD your God will set you high above all the nations on earth. All these blessings will come on you and accompany you if you obey the LORD your God...You will lend to many nations but will borrow from none" (Deuteronomy 28:1-2,12).

- Being in debt is considered a curse. "If you do not obey the LORD your God and do not carefully follow all his commands and decrees I am giving you today, all these curses will come on you and overtake you…The foreigners who reside among you will rise above you higher and higher, but you will sink lower and lower. They will lend to you, but you will not lend to them. They will be the head, but you will be the tail" (Deuteronomy 28:15,43-44).

- Debt is considered slavery. "The rich rule over the poor, and the borrower is slave to the lender" (Proverbs 22:7). Anyone who has been burdened by debt understands the truth of this verse.

Although the Bible discourages the use of debt, debt is not necessarily a sin. There is a difference between a command and a principle. A principle is an instruction from the Lord to help guide our decisions. Commands are laws that must be followed. Consequences may follow from ignoring a principle, but punishment will follow as a result of ignoring God's commands. Following God's principles is more beneficial than worldly wisdom.

But not all debt is bad. Debt creates a state of slavery when the borrower is obligated to pay others to the point where the freedom to decide where to spend income no longer exists. At that point debt is controlling the circumstances rather than the person controlling the debt.

What Is Good Debt?

Good debt is any debt that creates value or generates income in the long term, such as home ownership, student loans, real estate mortgages, and the like. Even home equity loans and credit cards can be good debt if they are used wisely to buy assets that appreciate versus depreciate—and have low interest rates.

What Is Bad Debt?

Bad debt is using credit you cannot afford to purchase things that quickly lose their value. Bad debt often has a high interest rate, which is offered to those who have bad credit. Charging a $200 dress on an

18% credit card is bad debt unless you can afford to pay it off before the next billing cycle.

Other bad debt includes cash advances, payday loans, pawnshops, and rent-to-own establishments. They all make their money off of desperate people who are willing to pay excessive interest rates. They tempt the buyer with low weekly payments that seem to drag on and on for an eternity.

Here's the bottom line regarding the danger of debt: It often mortgages the future. Any future income must now be used to pay off the debt instead of being used for savings or investments. In Luke 12:15, Jesus gives a word of caution: "Watch out! Be on your guard against all kinds of greed; life does not consist in an abundance of possessions." This can be hard to live by in our society, where everyone has the latest cell phone, tablet, car, or gadget. But the caution is worth heeding. All of us must learn to recognize and avoid the desire for instant gratification. Yes, the fear of missing out is real and advertisers, retailers, and creditors all want our money. We must take control of our spending and learn to say no more often than we say yes.

Integrity in Borrowing

As stated earlier, debt itself is not a sin, but running up so much debt that you can't make your monthly payments is a sin. All women of God should be known as people of honesty and integrity. In Psalm 37:21, God says, "The wicked borrow and do not repay." What is borrowed must be repaid. Walking in integrity means that if you borrow money to buy a car, house, or any other item, you must make every effort to pay it back according to the agreement. "It is better that you should not vow than that you should vow and not pay" (Ecclesiastes 5:5 ESV).

If you have already messed up in this area, all is not lost. This isn't a call to beat yourself up for getting behind on payments. Instead, thank God for His grace and mercy. Repent and ask for God's intervention in your finances and begin to do whatever you can to pay everyone you owe.

But remember to set priorities. Take care of your necessities first.

Don't let threatening phone calls from creditors make you send them the money you need for basic necessities such as your shelter or transportation. You must prioritize until you get your spending under control. When putting together a plan to pay your creditors, be honest about what you can realistically afford and then faithfully stand by that promise.

Payment of existing financial obligations may seem impossible right now, but be encouraged. God will honor your decision to be a woman of integrity. And He has a plan for your provision...no matter who you are.

First Kings 17 relates the story of a starving single parent. She had one last meal that she planned to cook for herself and her son, and then she was prepared for them both to die. But the prophet Elijah asked her to feed him first. "She went away and did as Elijah had told her. So there was food every day for Elijah and for the woman and her family. For the jar of flour was not used up and the jug of oil did not run dry" (verse 15-16).

In another situation, in 2 Kings 4, a widow's deceased husband left behind debts, and his creditors were soon coming to take her two sons as collateral. When she told Elisha about it, he asked what she had in the house, but all she had was a small jar of olive oil. Elisha instructed her to borrow as many jars as she could from her neighbors and to pour her oil into all of them until they were filled. She was able to fill every jar she had borrowed from the one jar of oil she had. Finally, the oil stopped flowing. "She went and told the man of God, and he said, 'Go, sell the oil and pay your debts. You and your sons can live on what is left'" (verse 7). God is the same yesterday, today, and forever. He can give you a creative way to get out of debt.

Ways to Eliminate Debt

Often people have good intentions but no idea how to begin to become debt free. Here are some practical ways to get started.

Stop Borrowing

People in debt often pile on more debt in order to make ends meet, but that's not a viable solution, as it only compounds the problem. The only way to get debt under control is to stop adding to it. It may require a level of discipline that you have never exercised, but with God's help, all things are possible.

Begin Saving

This probably seems like meaningless advice for those deep in debt. How can anyone save when they don't have the money to pay their bills? It's simple. People in debt are often in the habit of wasting money, even if it's a small amount here and there, on daily lattes, fast food, movies, etc. The average person can begin to save $5 a week. The important thing is to start somewhere and save whatever is available, even if it's only a few cents. Even pennies eventually become dollars.

Seek Help

Not everyone can do it alone. Often churches have a credit counseling program or offer a course like Dave Ramsey's *Financial Peace University* (*daveramsey.com/FPU*) or Crown's *Money Life* (*crown.org*). Both courses are also available for personal purchase if you want to work through the material on your own.

In addition to programs through the church, other organizations offer programs to help the public get their finances in shape. Here are just a few of the services available:

- *Credit Counseling:* Credit counseling agencies review your budget, evaluate debt-repayment alternatives, and suggest solutions. Their employees are professionals who are certified to teach you the basic skills necessary to restore financial health. Always do your research and check the Internet for possible complaints against the company before you commit to using their services. Simply go to *Google.com* and type in "complaints against (name)."

  The mere act of getting credit counseling will not affect your credit score. However, when the agency negotiates lower rates or payments and remits your payments to your creditors as part of a debt management plan, there may be a note on your credit report. But if you pay according to the plan, there should be no impact on your credit score.

- *Debt Management:* The goal of debt management is to eliminate debt by reducing interest rates and fees, as well as lowering the monthly payment. *You are still liable for the full amount owed, but you can make payments at a level most affordable for your situation.* This is a good option because it doesn't negatively affect your credit score; in fact, your score will increase because you are consistently making payments on time. This option will likely cost you a maintenance fee. Once you choose this plan, it's best to stick with it; otherwise, you may lose the arrangements made on your behalf to repay the debt.

- *Debt Consolidation:* Debt consolidation lenders advance you money to pay off your debts. You then pay the loan company a lower monthly amount, effectively combining your many debts into one and lowering your overall interest rate. Debt consolidation experts have special relationships with lenders and will work with you to find one that suits your budget. Not everyone qualifies for debt consolidation because it is often dependent on the borrower's credit score. Also, be sure to find out how the consolidation will affect secured assets such as your house or car. The lender will surely require collateral.

- *Debt Settlement:* In a debt-settlement program, the credit counseling agency helps you work with lenders to settle your debt for less than the total amount owed, often 50 to 80 percent less. This isn't the best option for those with moderate to good credit, *as it will likely reduce your credit score.* The fact that you didn't pay the full balance may be reflected on your credit report. And if you have been late in making payments, those will remain on your report as well.

- *Bankruptcy:* This is a last resort, but it can be helpful because it essentially wipes the slate clean and rids you of most debt. There are two types of individual bankruptcy: Chapter 7 cancels your debts; Chapter 13 puts you on a three- to five-year payment plan to pay off your debts. Filing bankruptcy often allows you to keep assets such as your home, car, clothing, and retirement savings. But bankruptcy will lower your credit score and can stay on your credit report for seven to ten years. *Also, some debts, such as student loans, child support, alimony, and back taxes, cannot be eliminated.*

The blessings of becoming debt-free go far beyond the financial benefits. As Howard Dayton, co-founder of Crown Financial Ministries and former host of the *Money Matters* radio show, put it, "No one who is financially bound can be spiritually free."[1]

Here is how one young lady found freedom.

Edna's Story: Escape from Student Loan Prison

I graduated from a public college in 2011 with $38,000 in outstanding student loans. My first career position paid $50,000, which was about 20 percent below the current market rate. I accepted the position because I just wanted a job. After two years of faithful loan payments against the ten-year agreement, I had only reduced the loan balance by $2,000. I became totally frustrated. No way was I going to spend ten years paying off my educational debt. I made a conscious decision not to bring debt from my twenties into my thirties. I researched loan consolidation programs and found one that worked for my loan types.

Then the real sacrifice began. I live in Los Angeles where the cost of living is quite high. So the first thing I did was to get a roommate. This was especially hard as I am an introvert. We moved to a modest apartment in the less-fashionable part of the city. Earplugs and patience were my key tools. These actions enabled me to pay six times the scheduled monthly payment on the loan. Now I was making significant reductions of the balance. Seeing that balance go down motivated me to make more sacrifices. I decided I would drive my 2007 auto until the wheels fell off.

I shopped at less expensive grocery stores, got most of my entertainment from the library, and threatened to cancel my cable/Internet service every time my "promotional" pricing ended—a ploy that prompted the customer service agent to reactivate my promotion. Every year I would allocate half of my tax refund to reducing my student loans. I split the remainder between savings and spending. Giving myself the spending allowance prevented me for making impulsive purchases. I also took on a couple of side jobs during the year.

Now, just a mere six years after getting my degree, my loans are paid in full—four years ahead of the ten-year repayment plan. I have no other debt, so every dollar I make is all truly mine! Living like no one else does for the last several years has enabled me to live like no one else can long-term. As my pastor says, "If you do what others won't do, you can have what others can't have." Aggressive debt payment is hard and requires discipline, but it is so rewarding in the end.

Control Your Credit Utilization Ratio

The formula for calculating your credit utilization ratio is pretty straightforward. To figure it out for an individual credit card, divide your card balance by your total credit limit. FICO suggests that a good debt-to-credit ratio percentage is below 30 percent and that goes for the ratio on any one of your credit cards individually as well as for your overall ratio for all of them combined. Consider this example for clarity.

Card	A Outstanding Balance	B Credit Limit	A / B Credit Utilization
A	$800	$1,500	53%
B	$900	$3,000	30%
C	$200	$5,500	4%
TOTAL	$600	$10,000	6%

Now let's say you have three credit cards with credit limits of $1,000, $3,500 and $5,000. To determine your overall credit utilization, first compute your total combined credit limits ($9,500). Next, divide your total balance across all three cards by the sum of your credit limits. If you have $200 outstanding balance on each of the three cards, your debt-to-credit ratio would be approximately six percent ($600 divided by $9,500)—well below the recommended average.

Part 2

CLEAR YOUR EMOTIONAL HURDLES

6

FORSAKE FALSE RESPONSIBILITY

Money Mentoring Moment

Assuming responsibility for obligations that should be fulfilled by others will keep you financially and emotionally frustrated.

Marsha was in tears. I was somewhat surprised to receive a call from her since our only interaction had been at an office where I had met her while consulting on the finances of a nonprofit organization. I knew that she had recently left that organization for a golden opportunity at a growing company. However, it was clear something was terribly wrong.

Marsha: Hi, Deborah. I'm calling because I knew you would be just the person to tell me how to respond to my dilemma. I love my new job at X Company, and the 30 percent pay raise they gave me has made a big difference in the quality of my life. I have moved into a nicer apartment and am saving money. I love the people I work with, and my boss has already started talking about a promotion even though I've only been here a few months.

Me: Wow! Sounds great! So what's the problem?

Marsha: Well, I got a call from my old boss today. He wants me to come back. He tried hiring a couple of folks from an employment agency to replace me, but they have not worked out. Actually, I heard they were quite competent, but they couldn't adjust to management's chaotic style so they quit. I feel I should help out, but I really don't want to go back to that environment. I worked long hours in cramped quarters, received few benefits, and got little appreciation for all the effort I put in. I'm happy where I am. I'm on a good career track.

Me: Whoa, Marsha. I'm confused. Tell me why you feel it's your responsibility to rescue your former employer because the executive director has created an environment that new hires find intolerable.

Marsha: Well, I was the go-to person when I worked there. You have to understand that I was an emotional wreck when the director hired me 20 years ago. He gave me a chance and a lot of support. I know sometimes he can be a little demanding and insensitive to the needs of the employees, but I can't abandon him now when he needs me the most. It just doesn't seem right to say no.

Marsha was suffering a case of *false responsibility*—assuming responsibility for the shortcomings, bad judgment, irresponsible actions, and dilemmas of others. I can't begin to tell you how many "Marshas" I have met over the decades. Sometimes she is the church administrator who becomes the go-to person for virtually everything. She is often the loyal company employee who always steps in to take up the slack for those who don't fulfill their role in meeting key deadlines. She is frequently the oldest (or most responsible) female in a large family and has succumbed to the expectations of others. She finds herself organizing (and maybe even financing) all holiday, birthday, and other family celebrations—with little support from others.

The Blind Spot

False responsibility is such a blind spot to the sufferer that it often takes the intervention of others to shine a light on it. It can have a huge impact on your work life, your finances, and your health. I've been there.

In May 2012, my 82-year-old mother collapsed as I was taking her downstairs for breakfast. I called the paramedics, but I decided that rather than riding in the ambulance with her, I'd drive my car to the hospital so that I would have transportation back home later that day. With a book manuscript deadline looming, I took a few extra minutes to grab my laptop computer so that I could continue to write while I waited for her to get medical attention. I had experienced this routine before with various relatives. When I arrived at the hospital, I learned that the ambulance had been rerouted to another medical facility. By the time I arrived at the new hospital, she had passed away. There are no words more difficult to hear than a doctor's somber announcement that a beloved relative has passed away.

For several years I took responsibility for her dying without a single family member being present. *If only I hadn't been so concerned about completing my book, Mom wouldn't have died alone.* The guilt was so great it interfered with my ability to write, to focus, and to be creative. Family and friends reminded me that God orchestrates the events of all our lives and that it was obviously not His will for me to see my mother make the transition from life to death. By the grace of God, I have finally let go of the false guilt. The evil one, the accuser, can no longer use it to threaten my progress or my peace.

What I learned from this experience is that we should seek to understand what we are truly responsible for and what we are not—in relational and financial matters. When tempted to take responsibility for something that may not be our obligation, we need to ask three critical questions:

- Did I play a role in *creating* these circumstances?
- Did I have any *control* over the circumstances that led to this situation?

- Do I sense a divine *call* to fix this situation or is this a self-imposed expectation?

Self-Analysis in Action

Allison loves her family very much—especially her nephews and nieces.

Several years ago, her brother, Jeff, and his fiancée, Dawn, had a baby out of wedlock. Jeff was furious because he felt Dawn was not qualified to be a mother. When Baby Karla was born, Jeff had very little interaction with her for the first six months of her life. He didn't hold her or show any kind of affection.

Since Karla was her niece, Jeff's sister felt responsible to show her the love that Jeff refused to extend to her. She showered the baby with gifts that she couldn't afford in an effort to make up for Jeff's behavior. She convinced herself that if she didn't do these things, the baby would be emotionally scarred the rest of her life. Now for Allison's three-question analysis:

- Did she play a role in *creating* these circumstances? Certainly not!
- Did Allison have any *control* over the circumstances that led to Baby Karla's birth? No!
- Was God *calling* Allison to fix this situation? Nope!

Allison's false responsibility and self-imposed expectations drove her to go beyond what she was obligated to do. I know that this is common behavior among women, but as we head toward financial empowerment, we must stop and deal with the emotional issues that derail our finances. Again, false responsibility is usually a blind spot to the sufferer. Therefore, it is critical that you have a friend who has the courage to confront you about your self-defeating behavior. Don't brush their input aside. Remember that nobody has 20-20 vision on themselves. Nobody. Including me. And you.

Thank God that Moses had his caring father-in-law Jethro to alert him to the fact that he had taken on too much responsibility for the

Jewish multitude he had led out of Egypt. After their exodus, Jethro reunited Moses with his wife and two sons in the desert. When he saw Moses taking responsibility for settling even the smallest of disputes among the people, he exclaimed, "The thing that you do is not good" (Exodus 18:17 NKJV). He went on to suggest a leadership structure that would give delegated responsibility to other leaders for settling minor disputes. Moses was humble enough to listen. The plan worked. Yes, God had called him to be the deliverer, but He was not calling him to be deluged with the day-to-day minor conflicts.

Letting Go

You may be thinking, *Okay, I've completed my three-question self-analysis, but how do I stop engaging in this kind of behavior? People have become accustomed to me doing what I do. This may create tension in my relationships.* You are absolutely right. Your actions have taught others what to expect from you, and a change may not go over very well. It's time to teach them a different lesson now. I like to take the A-B-C approach to problem solving:

> **A:** Acknowledge the real problem. Call it what it is—false responsibility. Also acknowledge the subtle satisfaction you get out of being the "savior" in the situation.

> **B:** Believe that God will give you the grace (divine enablement) to do what you have to do.

> **C:** Change your actions, starting with baby steps.

Here are a couple of scenarios with suggested scripts to get you started:

Scenario 1 (Workplace): Ted, your coworker, took a long lunch at work and has to leave early for a special occasion. In typical fashion, he won't be able to complete his part of the departmental project by tomorrow's deadline. He asks if you will be a "doll" and do it for him.

Solution: Without emotion or a negative attitude, you simply say to him, "Oh, Ted, I have a commitment too. I'm sorry I can't accommodate you." Do not add the words "this time"; that leaves the door open for a future request. Always, always have "another commitment"—even if you do not have a scheduled appointment with someone. You have not lied; you do indeed have a "commitment"…to yourself…to stop assuming false responsibility! Do not offer an extended explanation; you are not obligated to justify your personal decisions to a co-worker.

Scenario 2 (Family): Mother's Day is approaching, but none of your five siblings has mentioned any plans for celebrating with your mother. You have taught them by your past actions that you will assume that responsibility. You are holding out for one of them to make a suggestion. As late as the Saturday night before the big day, no one has come forth. On Sunday morning, you get a call from your sister. "Hey, what are we doing for Mom today?"

Solution: You pleasantly reply, "I'm going to take her to church and then to lunch afterward. Do you want to join us?" If the other siblings call, use the same script. Short and sweet. And for goodness' sake, do not feel obligated to pay for anyone's meal other than your mother's—even if you are the only sibling who can afford it. You can choose to treat your family at a later event if you feel so inclined. But refrain for now; you are teaching them that you will be playing a different role going forward.

False Responsibility Versus True Responsibility

Based on the foregoing discussion, you may be tempted to conclude that I'm suggesting you become selfish, unhelpful, and confrontational. Nothing could be farther from the truth. There are situations in our lives where we do indeed have true (versus false) responsibility.

- We are responsible for honoring our parents and making sure we do our part in ensuring their basic needs are met;

however, we are not obligated to be the totality of their social life. They have to accept responsibility for reaching out to others and should not try to manipulate us into spending all our available time with them and putting our husband and children in second place.

- We are responsible for helping the needy when we have the resources to do so. "If someone has enough money to live well and sees a brother or sister in need but shows no compassion—how can God's love be in that person?" (1 John 3:17 NLT). Sometimes it's hard to make the distinction between someone being "needy" and our need to be needed. This is where we have to go back and not only do the three-question self-analysis, but also allow God to direct our actions.

- As parents, we are responsible for teaching our children the ways of God; however, when they become adults, they may need our wise counsel, but they don't need to be parented. We are not obligated to make them attend church, marry the ideal person we have selected, or rescue them from their unwise financial decisions.

As women, we wear many hats. Before we jump in and save the day, we need to realize that just because we *can* do something doesn't mean that God is *calling* us to do it. I repeat: *Can is not a call.* Saying no or relinquishing certain self-imposed obligations can be scary. Don't let the fear of rejection or alienation stop you from shifting responsibility back to others when the burden should be theirs.

We must discern the leading of the Spirit as we pray the "Serenity Prayer": "God, grant me the serenity to accept the things I cannot change, courage to change the things I can, and wisdom to know the difference."

ELIMINATE EMOTIONAL EXPENDITURES

Money Mentoring Moment

Every financial decision is rooted in a positive or negative emotion; therefore, you will want to become self-aware enough to recognize when you may be on the slippery slope of your emotions creating a financial problem.

t is said that managing finances is 90 percent emotions and 10 percent logic. Truth is, all spending is based on an emotion—even positive spending often done out of love, appreciation, or gratitude. Negative emotional spending takes place when we spend money because we are unhappy with some aspect of our life. We may engage in this kind of spending for reasons including fear, insecurity, boredom, stress, loneliness, anger, and a host of other negative feelings.

Recognize the Signs

Here are six red flags to watch out for to avoid emotional spending:[1]

1. Seeking a high through shopping to get instant gratification.

2. Telling yourself you deserve to make the buy.

3. Spending even when you're worried about money or debt.

4. Shopping as a response to a stressful event in your life.

5. Spending to try to keep up with the Joneses.

6. Shopping with the intention of returning items.

Spending money seems to ease the bad feelings these emotions bring about, but here's the problem: The solution is temporary. After you've made your purchase and the emotional high wears off, those feelings come rushing back because you haven't dealt with the root of the problem.

Emotional spending temporarily restores balance to our lives. We spend money to regulate our emotions—we feel down, but we want to feel up. Emotion regulation is the process of controlling how and when to express your emotions. The part of the brain that regulates emotions is the prefrontal cortex. You activate the prefrontal cortex when you regulate your emotions. When you fail to do so, the limbic system takes control. The limbic system causes us to react impulsively. It doesn't care about logic, just about feelings. Fortunately, the prefrontal cortex can overpower the limbic system. And that's good news for those who are prone to emotional spending.

But how can we redirect the control of one part of the brain to the other? It all starts with self-awareness. For example, what is the most frequent advice people give when you are angry? That's right, count to ten! In fact, we hear that advice so much that it sounds trite, but the exercise is actually a direct activation of the prefrontal cortex. You become aware that you are angry, and in acknowledging that anger, you count to ten to give yourself time to calm down. (Now, some of you may need to count to one thousand, but the principle is the same!) And you can use the count-to-ten method for anything, including calming yourself down before deciding to spend impulsively. It's also a good idea to deeply inhale and exhale "Jesus" or "Peace" when attempting to calm your emotions.

This self-awareness is the key to controlling impulsive spending. Consider the following scenarios:

Scenario 1: You're sitting on the couch watching TV and feeling blue. You think, *If I just go down to the mall and get that pair of shoes I wanted, I will feel better.* So you get up, turn off the TV, and head for the mall. Several hours later, you're back home on the same couch, with the same feelings, but now you also have a new pair of $100 shoes you couldn't afford. You felt good while you were buying them, but nothing has changed fundamentally, which is why the bad feelings returned.

Scenario 2: You're sitting on the couch watching TV and feeling blue. You think, *If I just go down to the mall and get that pair of shoes I want, I will feel better.* But then you allow the prefrontal cortex to do its work, and you become aware that your desire to shop is an unhealthy way of dealing with your feelings. This self-awareness causes you to wonder, *What can I do to productively improve my mood besides shop?*

So you get up, turn off the TV, and head for the gym. Several hours later, you're back home. This time you're at your desk, knocking out a few pages of a book you desire to finish soon, or you're clearing out that closet you've been meaning to get to. And you feel amazing, for many reasons:

- Exercise releases endorphins, which work to naturally improve your mood and decrease stress.

- You feel good because you know exercising will improve your health.

- Your self-esteem is enhanced because you made a good decision when you could have made a bad one.

- Going home and doing something productive further enhances your self-esteem and makes you feel even better about yourself.

And remember, all of these good things occurred because of the one simple decision to go to the gym instead of the mall. That's the power of the prefrontal cortex at work.

The Importance of Doing a Self-Audit

Now, our Scenario #2 above was great, but going to the gym didn't solve the whole problem. It didn't get to the underlying heart of your emotions. If you were just bored, you don't need to evaluate any further. You did something that made you feel good and productive, and that effectively solved the problem of boredom.

But what if you were sad about a fight with a friend, have low self-esteem issues, or just feel depressed about your life? As we spend money, we must have the courage to do a self-audit and admit what emotion is driving our spending. Our emotions need to be dealt with, but we can only do that when we are honest about identifying the underlying emotion and determining what we need to do to get back in balance.

Psalm 51:6 tells us that God desires "truth in the inward parts" (NKJV). God wants us to embrace truth, but truth without the knowledge to make improvements can be depressing. However, the second part of the verse also promises God will give us wisdom concerning that truth: "In the hidden part You will make me to know wisdom" (NKJV). Now, that's great news.

Money and possessions were never meant to be the solution for our emotional health. The Bible is filled with warnings about money:

- "Why spend money on what is not bread, and your labor on what does not satisfy?" (Isaiah 55:2). We often spend money on things that are not necessities and time on things that are not productive.

- "Whoever loves money never has enough; whoever loves wealth is never satisfied with their income" (Ecclesiastes 5:10). Those who are consumed with the love of money are often greedy. They will continue chasing material things, and regardless of how much they accumulate, nothing will ever truly satisfy them.

- "For we brought nothing into the world, and we can take
  nothing out of it" (1 Timothy 6:7). When we have a proper
  view of money and possessions, we understand that nothing we buy will come with us when we die. It all stays right
  here. That should put things into perspective the next time
  the urge comes to purchase something that you know you
  shouldn't.

Do a self-audit to evaluate your mind-set on money and possessions. Remember that beliefs dictate behavior. As the saying goes, "Free
your mind and the rest will follow."

The Addictive Nature of Emotional Spending

The obvious side effect of emotional spending is using money you
don't have and going deeper into a financial hole. However, another
side effect is the possibility of addiction. Many people are addicted to
shopping but fail to acknowledge it as an addiction. Those who do
acknowledge it as such think of it as a "safe" or acceptable addiction—
better than alcohol, drugs, or sex.

But we must remember that when we occupy ourselves to the point
of obsession with anything other than God, it becomes an idol. The
apostle Paul summed it up best:

> All things are lawful [that is, morally legitimate, permissible],
> but not all things are beneficial or advantageous. All things
> are lawful, but not all things are constructive [to character]
> and edifying [to spiritual life] (1 Corinthians 10:23 AMP).

Paul is obviously talking here about those gray areas that are not
directly called sin. Many times as Christians, we try to find out how
much we can get away with—how close we can get to the line before
we are considered in violation of God's laws. For example, we know
it would be wrong to take the family rent and blow it on a new wardrobe. But we justify using a credit card to buy an expensive pair of shoes
(when we already have too much debt) because we think, *What's a little more debt added to the mountain that already exists?*

But Paul brings it all into perspective. We should avoid anything that is not beneficial. And we should certainly say no to anything that has control over us, anything that has brought us under its power. And that's the mind-set you must have about spending. If you can't control it, you are under its power, and that is no way for a woman of God to live.

Tips to Avoid Impulsive Spending

Even after you identify the emotions (anger, disappointment, rejection, and the like) that lead to impulsive spending, breaking that habit is easier said than done. Until you master the denial of those impulses, here are some helpful guidelines to follow:

- Leave your credit cards at home. Perhaps you can't resist the urge to go to the store, but maybe you have enough willpower to at least take your credit cards out of your purse before you leave. This will force you to spend only the money you have on hand rather than going further into debt.

- Shop online instead of going to the store. There's something about being inside the store that fuels our impulse to purchase. We may go to the store with good intentions to buy only what we need, but along the way other things call out to us to at least stop and have a look. And that "innocent" look leads to a purchase. In an online store, you can just search for what you need and get out of there. Just make sure you don't browse everything they have to offer or you'll be tempted to overspend.

- Distract yourself. There are many things you can do instead of going to the store. Make a list of those things before you have a bad day, and you can draw upon them when you need to. The list can include such things as going to the gym, reading a book, watching a good movie, and visiting a friend. The key is to do something that will make you feel good without a high price tag.

Being Content

On a scale of 1 to 10, how content are you with your life? Being content means you are satisfied with the status quo until God moves you to the next chapter. Discontentment is often at the heart of emotional spending. Learning the art of contentment can help you overcome this detrimental attitude.

The Scriptures are full of admonitions to practice contentment. First Timothy 6:6-8 tells us that "godliness with contentment is great gain. For we brought nothing into the world, and we can take nothing out of it. But if we have food and clothing, we will be content with that." Similarly, in Matthew 6:25, Jesus tells us not to worry about food and clothing. He further admonishes us to "seek first his kingdom and his righteousness, and all these things will be given to you as well" (verse 33).

The apostle Paul experienced every kind of trial imaginable. He was beaten, imprisoned, stoned, shipwrecked, constantly in danger, had trouble sleeping, and often went without food and water. Yet he learned to be content, saying, "I have learned in whatever situation I am to be content. I know how to be brought low, and I know how to abound. In any and every circumstance, I have learned the secret of facing plenty and hunger, abundance and need. I can do all things through him who strengthens me" (Philippians 4:11-13 ESV).

Can you learn to be content in any situation? If Paul could, anyone can. And it's the secret to learning how to eliminate emotional expenditures. Whatever you have, consider it enough until God brings you something better. Being content doesn't mean we don't want something better. It doesn't mean we never strive to improve. But it does mean that until I get there, I am okay. I am satisfied.

Emotional spending is a problem, and the only way we can deal with it is to see it as such. This is the first step to resolving the issue. Your emotions should never be allowed to control you. Instead, with the help of the Holy Spirit, you can exert control over your emotions. Lean and depend on God to help you learn to be content.

8

END FINANCIAL ENABLING

Money Mentoring Moment

*When we enable others, we sabotage their personal
development, prevent them from reaping the
consequences of their negative behavior, and create
emotional and financial stress for ourselves.*

J ulie was born out of wedlock to a teen mom during her senior
year in high school. Her father, while not denying his paternity,
ran away to the army and refused to provide any support for her.
Her grandmother, unable to bear the rejection of her precious grand-
daughter, stepped in and made sure that little Julie never lacked for
anything. Granny gave her a credit card when she was in her early teens.
Julie never even saw the monthly statements; she only made charges.
Granny also purchased her school clothes from one of the most expensive retail stores in town.

Needless to say, Julie developed into a full-fledged spoiled brat.
Later, she met a young man and they got married. But the marriage
failed when he could no longer deal with the financial chaos she created.

Julie's work history has been rocky. She has never completed the
training or education necessary to get a stable job and become financially independent. She brags that she is "high maintenance," and any
man who comes into her life must understand that and be prepared
to deal with it.

I wish this story had a happy ending. Years later, Julie's ailing grandmother continues to subsidize her rent and other basic expenses. She complains about it and often finds herself in a financial bind, unable to purchase her medication because she "has to" help Julie. As long as Granny is alive and functioning in her role as chief enabler, Julie will continue in the cycle of receiving destructive support and engaging in destructive financial behavior.

Parental Enabling

One of my mentors would often say, "Where we stand usually depends on where we sit." I don't have children, so I'm going to tread lightly here since I do not sit in the seat of a mother. However, I have six brothers, and I've had a front-row seat in observing what it looks like when a mother enables a son.

My mom, now deceased, struggled financially as a single parent; her boys were her world. They gave her the validation that my dad was not emotionally capable of giving during their marriage. Her sons also met a key need in her life—her need to be needed, loved, and affirmed. The thought of losing them made her critical of their girlfriends and significant others.

When one son battled drugs and finally decided to seek help, she balked at the tough-love and boundary-setting strategies the drug counselor suggested during the family support sessions. She later complained, "Those people are just trying to teach you to be mean to your kids." The "kid" was over 40 years old! Now, five years after her death, the "kid" is finally starting to take responsibility for his life and has stopped the bailout calls to his siblings. Oh, that she could have sought God's grace to say no to the endless enabling—making temporary cash advances that always became permanent, allowing grown men to live under her roof without paying rent or other household costs, lending her car that was always returned with an empty gas tank, and on and on it went. While she in no way condoned the negative or irresponsible behavior, she never wanted it to appear to her kids or others that she did not love and support them. She never made the distinction between constructive help and destructive help. Like many parents, she also felt she had no choice but to enable the drug-addicted son. She feared that if she set boundaries with consequences, he would end up on the streets and ultimately die there.

Ending the Enabling

One of the key strategies for ending financial enabling is to require your adult child to participate in their financial survival and well-being by assuming assigned responsibilities. The story of the nameless widow in 2 Kings 4 is a great example. (You met her in chapter 5, "Master Your Debts," but there is even more to the story.) Her husband had been a student in Elisha's school of the prophets. Although a God-fearing man, he died with outstanding debts that she had no way of repaying. The creditors were threatening to take her two sons as slaves to satisfy the obligation.

In her distress, she sought the counsel of Elisha. He asked her the same question we all need to consider when we face a financial crisis:

> "Tell me, what do you have in the house?" [In other words, "What do you have to work with?"]
>
> "Nothing at all, except a flask of olive oil," she replied.
>
> And Elisha said, "Borrow as many empty jars as you can from your friends and neighbors. Then go into your house with your sons and shut the door behind you. Pour olive oil from your flask into the jars, setting each one aside when it is filled."
>
> So she did as she was told. Her sons kept bringing jars to her, and she filled one after another. Soon every container was full to the brim!
>
> "Bring me another jar," she said to one of her sons.
>
> "There aren't any more!" he told her. And then the olive oil stopped flowing.
>
> When she told the man of God what had happened, he said to her, "Now sell the olive oil and pay your debts, and you and your sons can live on what is left over" (verses 2-7 NLT).

Notice the number of references to her "sons" in this passage. Yes, they played a key role in securing their freedom from the creditors. No enabling mother in this story!

How Women Can Stop Enabling

People use the term *enabler* with a bit of disdain when describing such individuals. However, to their credit, their goals for being so are noble. They simply are trying to help someone they care about. I believe that enabling is a mercy gift taken to the extreme. Fear not, you can find the balance. Consider these suggestions:

- Get real about your emotional payoff of being needed. Yes, it feels good to solve a problem and to think we are adding value to someone's life, but enabling does the opposite; it devalues.

- Understand the consequences and detriment of enabling others. It can lower their self-esteem and cause them to remain dependent on the enabler. It can also encourage them to underperform, as well as resent and resist those who attempt to hold their feet to the fire in an effort to make them responsible.

- Assign the person an area of responsibility.

- By the grace of God, implement consequence if the responsibility is not met. "Those unwilling to work will not get to eat" (2 Thessalonians 3:10 NLT).

Peer-to-Peer Enabling

If you have frequently played the part of "Bailout Betty," you have taught the people in your circle of interaction to use you as their crutch—the classic role of the enabler. People may have become so used to you saying yes and supporting or excusing their bad behavior that they may protest your decision to end your enabling. Some may become angry, try to run a guilt trip on you for not accommodating their requests, or even abandon the relationship. Consider Marie's story:

My friend Glenda, a church leader, persuaded me to lend her the funds to pay off her car loan because she was being charged a significant amount of interest. She knew from experience that a loan from me would be interest-free. I reluctantly agreed. She prepared a contract that we both signed.

After making two payments, she decided she needed the money to put down a deposit on a mission trip to Africa. I told her she didn't have to make the next month's payment and to consider it as my contribution toward her trip. A month later, when the next payment was due, not only did she tell me she couldn't make it, but she asked me for a $1,200 loan to pay off the balance of the upcoming trip. She promised to pay both loans back as soon as she returned.

Over the next six months, Glenda only made a couple of payments against her obligations…and stopped talking to me. The $2,000 outstanding balance remains unpaid to this date. Since I have a signed promissory note, I could take her to small claims court, but I don't wish to do that. What really hurts me is to have lost her friendship. The truth is that I would have been okay with her repaying me whenever she could. Unfortunately, our friendship appears to be over.

Interestingly, Marie told me a few more personal stories with similar outcomes. She has a big heart but needs to make some key changes in her behavior if she wants to stop being an enabler. The most critical step is to become a broken record in saying no. "No" doesn't mean "I don't care about you." In fact, it can mean the exact opposite: "I care too much about you to assist you in continuing to be irresponsible."

What all enablers have in common is that they care about somebody who is out of control. The problem is that their desire to help is often greater than the person's desire to get help. Their refusal to exercise tough love creates personal stress and emotional pain. Many times enabled people demonstrate great resentment toward their enabler. Perhaps they are angry that they won't pull the plug and force them out of the pit of their irresponsibility.

When You Have Been "Enabled"

The bulk of our discussion has centered on the perils of being an enabler. However, what if you are a woman who has been enabled? How do you climb out of the pit and get on the path to a productive life? If you are reading this, I know there's a good chance that you desire to honor God with your life and embrace all that He has for you. Thus, you must always remember that you have a helper, the Holy Spirit. I offer the following steps. These are simple but may not be easy—but are always doable through the empowerment of the Holy Spirit.

1. Acknowledge that you have been a recipient of "destructive support."

2. Announce to your enablers that you desire to break the cycle.

3. Ask for their support and cooperation in helping you maintain your resolve.

4. Avoid discussing your financial situation with potential enablers.

5. Accept help only when it is required for necessities.

6. Accomplish small financial goals to stay motivated. For example, begin paying a certain utility bill if you live in the same house as your enabler, pay off a credit card balance, build an emergency reserve, etc.

7. Affirm your new status daily: *I am a mature adult who enjoys taking responsibility for my life. I'm standing on Galatians 6:5: "Every man shall bear his own burden"* (KJV).

Enabling is detrimental to the enabler and the enabled. It's time for both sides to recognize the problem and end it.

FIGHT THE FEARS OF FAILURE AND SUCCESS

Money Mentoring Moment

*Preparation is admirable and important. However,
when we allow our quest for perfection to keep us
from moving forward, we set up a shaky foundation
wherein we will ultimately rely on our qualifications
and skills rather than on the grace of God.*

Do you ever find yourself procrastinating when it comes to the big dreams you have for your life? Perhaps you've always wanted to write a book, become a public speaker, or get that promotion at work that only men seem to get. You want to be financially free, but more than that, you want enough money to do the really big things. The dreams are vivid in your imagination, yet somehow you seem to never take action to make your dreams a reality.

Procrastination is the assassinator of dreams. Procrastination is often seen as putting off something you don't want to do. While that is true, it doesn't address the real issue, that of why you don't want to do it. The foundation of most procrastination issues is fear, not laziness. What are you afraid of? Perhaps it is the fear of failure, the fear of success, or a combination of the two. Fear of failure is the irrational fear that you will not succeed. Specifically, it is the fear that you are not competent enough to reach a certain outcome. Other fears include fear of criticism and rejection. Here are some questions you may be asking yourself:

- What if I get that promotion and I can't live up to others' expectations of me?

- What if I become a famous author or speaker and my friends no longer talk me?

- What if success brings about too many changes in a life I've grown very comfortable with?

These are legitimate questions, but there is one more to consider: What if you fulfill your dreams and make enough money to begin to live a better life than you ever thought possible?

Done Versus Perfect

If you step out in faith and do the one thing that keeps you awake at night, a lot could go wrong. And this is the reality that often keeps you from moving forward. But it is better to see a project through to completion than to wait years and years until everything is perfect to start. Sometimes you just have to step out on faith and do the best you can. Don't get delayed or derailed with excess preparation. Some women take endless courses, year after year; wait to get their degree; wait until all the stars are perfectly aligned before they even begin to pursue their dreams. King Solomon was right. "Whoever watches the wind will not plant; whoever looks at the clouds will not reap" (Ecclesiastes 11:4). If you wait for perfect conditions, you will never get started. The time to act is now. The biblical writer James asked an interesting question: "What good is it, my brothers, if someone says he has faith but does not have works?" (James 2:14 ESV).

Sometimes you simply need to put feet to your faith. You must move from thinking about things, learning about things, and talking about things to actually doing them.

It's time to do whatever you must to accomplish your goals. Proverbs 23:23 instructs us to "buy" wisdom, instruction, and understanding. If you don't yet have all the skills you need, don't let that be a hindrance. Hire a coach or a professional consultant. Or you may need to dust off a skill that you've allowed to lie dormant. You know the familiar adage: "Use it or lose it."

What If You Fail?

Failure may seem like a negative word, but in reality it can act as a reset button. Failure isn't fatal. It provides the opportunity to start over and do things in a better way. We learn best from our mistakes. The questions we need to ask ourselves when facing failure are these:

1. Did I do anything to cause it?
2. Could I have done anything to prevent it?
3. Have I learned anything from it?
4. Will I do anything differently because of it?

The way to combat failure or the fear of incompetence is to draw on previous successes. Each success provides confidence for the next challenge. When David decided to fight Goliath, he related his past success to the doubting and fearful King Saul.

> But David said to Saul, "Your servant used to keep his father's sheep, and when a lion or a bear came and took a lamb out of the flock, I went out after it and struck it, and delivered the lamb from its mouth; and when it arose against me, I caught it by its beard, and struck and killed it. Your servant has killed both lion and bear; and this uncircumcised Philistine will be like one of them, seeing he has defied the armies of the living God" (1 Samuel 17:34-36 NKJV).

The more you take steps of faith and succeed, the more likely you are to move forward the next time and the less anxious you will be about failures.

Some of the most successful people have had a fear of failure. Men such as Steve Jobs, Bill Gates, and Tim Ferriss[1] and women like Oprah Winfrey. Steve Jobs failed to the point that he got kicked out of the company he started. But eventually he went back, and failed some more. But each failure brought him that much closer to establishing a company as strong as Apple. Jobs stated that he combated his fear of failure by remembering that one day he would die; in comparison, failure seemed like nothing. Bill Gates was a college dropout, and the first company he created failed. But he used his failure as a stepping-stone and learning experience to create Microsoft. In his book *Business @ the Speed of Thought: Succeeding in the Digital Economy*, he writes, "Once you embrace unpleasant news not as a negative but as evidence of a need for change, you aren't defeated by it. You're learning from it. It's all in how you approach failures."[2]

Tim Ferriss says the way he deals with his fears is to face them head-on. He created an exercise called fear-setting, which is much like goal-setting. He lists his fears, what could happen as a result of those fears, and what he can do to prevent an unfavorable outcome.[3]

Oprah Winfrey ran away from home at age 13, became pregnant, and lost the child at age 14. Her early years may have indicated to some that she would be a failure. But she turned her life around, went to college, and majored in communications. When the TV news show she was co-anchoring failed, Oprah felt she had failed as well. Still, she didn't give up. She learned from the experience that she enjoyed personal interest stories rather than hard news. She went on to do two successful hosting stints before she became famous and began hosting her namesake show. Today, she runs her own network.[4]

What If You Succeed?

We understand the fear of failure, but what about the fear of success? Oddly enough, this fear is often fueled by the same feelings of inadequacy and fear of failure. "What if people reject me?" "What if people criticize me?" We are afraid of finally arriving at our destination and not being able to maintain the success we sought.

Being successful is unfamiliar territory for some, and it often feels more comfortable to stay in the same place rather than embrace change. Things may not be as pleasant, but at least they are the same. Steve Pavlina discusses this problem as it relates to weight loss.[5] People see weight loss as generally a positive thing. Steve suggests realistically considering what will actually happen when we reach our goal (not what we hope will happen). Often on the road to success, unexpected side effects can subconsciously make us hesitate to move forward. Here are some of the side effects Steve gives for weight loss:

- People will notice and make comments.
- Other people will ask you for advice.
- You may feel the need to make a permanent lifestyle change to maintain your new weight.
- You may become more attractive to others and thereby attract more social encounters (wanted or unwanted).
- Friends might become jealous.
- Your family may resist your changes.
- You may feel stressed about whether you can maintain your new weight.

Ironically, many of these concerns are the same side effects that can occur if you become a financial success. Success is scary because it requires change, which has both positives and negatives attached. The fear of success is often unconscious; however, fears that are analyzed often lose their power when brought out into the light. But unacknowledged fears often get stronger and reinforce behaviors that keep us from working on the very goals that would bring us success.

If you suspect you have a fear of success, it's time to evaluate exactly what will happen if you succeed. Sometimes you will evaluate the side effects of your goal and realize that the negatives really do outweigh the positives, and you decide you don't want to pursue that goal after all. That's okay too; at least you've made an informed choice. The important thing is to face your fear of success head-on so you can make the appropriate decisions.

Fear is a bully. But like David, we can't let this giant defeat us. We must follow David's example and run toward it. Defeat is certain when we resist it.

Part 3

INCREASE
YOUR
CONFIDENCE

HONE YOUR PEOPLE SKILLS

Money Mentoring Moment

*Well-developed people skills equip you to
communicate positively, peacefully, and
productively; to understand the concerns and needs
of others; and to use such skills to solve problems
and meet personal and professional goals.*

We can always study more, obtain one more degree or certification, become a specialist in a new discipline, and make other attempts to increase our competency. Being skilled in whatever endeavor we pursue is a basic requirement if we want to succeed. In fact, King Solomon, the wisest king who ever lived, proclaimed, "If the ax is dull and its edge unsharpened, more strength is needed, but skill will bring success" (Ecclesiastes 10:10). Ironically, on the verge of his coronation as king of Israel, he did not cite the need for "more skills" when God appeared to him in a dream (1 Kings 3) and essentially offered him a blank check: "God said, 'What do you want? Ask, and I will give it to you!'" (verse 5 NLT).

Solomon wasted no time in responding.

> "Now, O LORD my God, you have made me king instead
> of my father, David, but I am like a little child who doesn't
> know his way around. And here I am in the midst of your

own chosen people, a nation so great and numerous they cannot be counted! Give me an understanding heart so that I can govern your people well and know the difference between right and wrong. For who by himself is able to govern this great people of yours?"

The Lord was pleased that Solomon had asked for wisdom. So God replied, "Because you have asked for wisdom in governing my people with justice and have not asked for a long life or wealth or the death of your enemies—I will give you what you asked for! I will give you a wise and understanding heart such as no one else has had or ever will have!" (verses 7-12 NLT).

Listen, ladies, technical skills may get you in the door, but good people skills are essential in moving you forward. And, they often determine the extent of your financial rewards. Whether you are teacher, a brain surgeon, an independent consultant, a law enforcement officer, or a homemaker, solid people skills will be one of the most empowering tools in your financial arsenal.

Avoid Self-Sabotage

My friend Lori related a story regarding how she'd hired "Debbie," a struggling single parent, to do ongoing computer consulting work for her budding company. Debbie was very competent but rather arrogant and displayed a superior attitude when it came to interacting with other staffers and consultants who were not as astute as she.

One day Lori informed her that she would personally tweak a certain software program to facilitate an upcoming mailing.

Debbie replied, "Well, that's not a good idea since you messed it up last time and I had to fix it!"

Lori was put off by the disrespectful tone, but rather than addressing it, she slowly began reducing the number of hours she required of Debbie—to the point that eventually she didn't "need" her services. What Lori really didn't "need" was Debbie disturbing her peace of mind. As a cash-strapped single parent, Debbie certainly needed the income, but her superior attitude and callous manner had sabotaged her financial well-being.

We must always be sensitive to how we relate to everybody in our circles of interaction—especially those who can influence our quality of life. This fact in no way minimizes the role God's grace and mercy can play in any situation. However, truth be told, we only have ourselves to blame in certain circumstances where better people skills would have avoided or solved the problem.

Indeed, it was the Egyptian maid Hagar's disrespectful attitude toward her Jewish mistress, Sarah, that led to a serious human resource problem. In her unwise attempt to help God fulfill His ten-year-old promise to give her husband a son, the barren Sarah convinced Abraham to sleep with Hagar. She explained, "Perhaps I can have children through her" (Genesis 16:2 NLT). Such was the custom of the day since Hagar was Sarah's property.

After Hagar became pregnant, she developed a disrespectful attitude toward Sarah. The Scriptures do not explain why, but we can conclude from her actions that she was unhappy with some aspect of the arrangement. However, the strong-willed, zero-tolerance Sarah was not going to stand for it, so she started treating her harshly. True to the meaning of her name, Hagar ("flight") ran away. She encountered an angel of the Lord in the wilderness who instructed her to go back and submit to Sarah's authority.

I've read several sermons and comments on this story and most of them portray Hagar as the helpless victim. I take issue with these conclusions. Hagar *chose* to disrespect Sarah, her employer; Sarah retaliated. They were both guilty of wrongdoing. However, Hagar, though she was young and fertile, stood to be the most economically disadvantaged as a result of her behavior. Although Sarah was old and barren, she was also rich and catered to by her husband, who loved her unconditionally. The moral of this aspect of the story and the goal of this chapter is to emphasize that operating from a platform of poor people skills is an unprofitable path.

Consider Your Behavior

Now let's look at some practical actions to avoid and some to embrace in order to sharpen your people skills. As you review this list, consider which skills you need to hone and which ones you can be grateful that the grace of God has prevailed in that area of your life.

1. *Smile.* Smiling is a universal language that never requires an interpreter. A smile will brighten your day as well as that of those you encounter. Of course, it's no effort to smile when things are going well, but sometimes we need to put the cart before the horse and smile even when things are not going well. Don't wait for joy to generate your smile; let your smile generate your joy. Never forget that feelings follow behavior; you will literally feel better when you smile. So just do it! Why not start right now?

2. *Engage common courtesies.* Say "Thank you," "Please," and "I'm sorry" to people in your personal and professional environments. Request rather than command or demand what you desire.

3. *Listen.* Be intentionally silent for periods of times during a conversation and make eye contact, nod, and listen. Ask clarifying questions as appropriate without accusing or prying. Show genuine interest in other people. Be conscious of the number of times you say "I" during your conversations. Don't allow the conversation to be all about you.

4. *Respect other people's right to believe, act, or dress differently.* No need to be adamant about non-eternal matters or those that do not affect the quality of your life. Keep your disdain and critical judgments to yourself. Do you really think that expressing them will change someone?

5. *Don't interrupt.* Even if the person is long-winded. If you feel you need to interject a point, raise your index finger slightly as if to ask for permission to speak. If that doesn't

work, just try to jump into the conversation at the end of a thought.

6. *Be quick to serve others.* Jesus cautioned His disciples, "The greatest among you must be a servant" (Matthew 23:11 NLT). Extend yourself to others as if you were serving God Himself—because you are! You will surely reap a positive reward.

7. *Be humble.* Humility is not an affected demeanor; it is a mind-set. Don't brag about your position, possessions, people you know, or places you've traveled. Doing so is a glaring indication of where you derive your self-worth from. Humility tops the chart as the most admired character trait; pride and arrogance are the most detestable.

8. *Resist envy.* If a family member, friend, co-worker, or acquaintance makes a notable achievement or acquires something of value, just congratulate her; don't compete or "hate." And for goodness' sake, don't mention another person who has exceeded her achievement. It will surely be perceived as your subtle attempt to level the playing field. You may as well plaster a sign on your forehead that reads, "Envy Alert!"

9. *Make every effort to remember people's names.* A person's name can be the sweetest and most important sound in any language. Recently I saw someone from our former church. By the grace of God, I remembered his name. He beamed as if I'd given him something valuable. Indeed, I had: significance.

10. *Always make the other person feel valued and appreciated.* Do it sincerely and without hidden motives. Phoniness is more discernable than you think. Simply acknowledge or praise people's small and large acts of service and accomplishments—especially your employees and family members.

11. *Don't gossip or reveal other people's secrets.* Your hearers
    or confidantes will most likely think, *She'll gossip about
    me next!* This is one of the fastest ways to lose credibility
    and gain a reputation for not having integrity. Refrain
    from passing on the negative comments that others have
    made about a person. What would be your purpose for
    disclosing such information in the first place?

12. *Don't whine.* There is no good outcome to whining and
    complaining. It will destroy your image as a problem
    solver or team player. If you must complain, do so only to
    those who can solve the problem.

13. *Be flexible and patient when unexpected situations arise.*
    Learning to go with the flow will increase your emotional
    and spiritual maturity—and avoid the harmful physical
    effects of unnecessary adrenalin rushes. Don't let your
    emotions hijack your peace and your ability to reason. The
    situation is "only a test." This too will pass.

14. *Resist showing partiality or prejudice.* The apostle James
    pulled no punches in declaring that discrimination or
    favoritism based on any and all outward factors (race,
    economic status, age, etc.) was a spiritual no-no: "But if
    you favor some people over others, you are committing
    a sin" (James 2:9 NLT). Even if you do indeed feel more
    favorably disposed to one person over the other, consider
    the sense of unfairness this creates in the non-preferred
    one and the damage it does to your spiritual foundation to
    live in rebellion against the Maker of all. Ask God for the
    grace to be fair always.

15. *Earn the right to give constructive criticism by consistently
    showing concern for other people's well-being.* Always give
    correction in private, and know that feedback is best
    received when it is requested. However, if you see someone
    going in the wrong direction, you have a scriptural

obligation to address it: "If another believer is overcome by some sin, you who are godly should gently and humbly help that person back onto the right path. And be careful not to fall into the same temptation yourself" (Galatians 6:1 NLT).

16. *Laugh.* Laugh at your shortcomings. Don't obsess with presenting an image of perfection. Others view perfect people as untouchable; imperfect people are relatable. Look for the humor in situations. Don't be the skunk at the picnic; be fun to interact with. People will notice and want to be around you. I can't begin to count the number of expensive social functions I have been invited to attend scot-free simply because the people said they wanted to sit at a fun table.

17. *Maintain a positive attitude.* Believe, according to Romans 8:28, that all things are working together for your good when you love God and are called according to His purpose. All things…nothing excluded.

18. *Admit your mistakes.* Trying to place blame on others will get you the label of "First Class Jerk." Be confident and humble enough to say, "I was wrong." It will increase rather than decrease your personal stock in the eyes of others.

19. *Establish, communicate, and honor clear boundaries.* No one is going to reject you for managing your life and career. You develop hostility and resentment toward others when you are upset with yourself for saying yes when you should have said no.

20. *Treat everyone with respect.* Subordinates. Children. Restaurant servers. Maintenance people. Assistants. Housekeepers. Everyone. There is never a justification for yelling, put-downs, threats, or other unkind behavior. A word to young people: Do not reprimand your

elders—that is, anybody old enough to be your parent. Do not take a disrespectful tone in expressing your feelings on a matter. You will most likely shoot yourself in the foot with them as they may write you off for consideration of future benefits and favors.

Just Do It!

The preceding behaviors can affect your finances. Although we were all born with a certain temperament, solid people skills are learned behavior. You do not have to change who you are. Even the most technically oriented or introverted woman can begin to incorporate people skills in her personal and professional settings. Don't feel pressured to become Chatty Cathy if you are more the Quiet Queenie type who prefers not to interact extensively with people. You will surely be happier if you chose a job or profession that is conducive to your temperament. For me, being an inspirational speaker fits my godly design. I love people, and I love empowering them with whatever I've learned—especially from the Word of God. On the other hand, my friend Billie, a counselor, is a great listener. She can sit and listen to people's problems for hours. I think I'm an okay listener, but honestly, I prefer folks to get to the point quickly so I can give them a recommendation or solution and go on to the next problem!

In the workplace, should your employer decide to make cutbacks during an economic slowdown, good people skills can often make it hard for them to terminate you. Smart managers know that having a friendly, helpful team player adds to the bottom line. The unspoken rule of business life is that people want to work with people they know, like, and trust.

So the challenge here is not about changing who you are but about coming to grips with the fact that whatever you desire in life will be achieved through people. Consequently, you must be mindful of behaviors and character traits that attract people and those that repel them.

Strongly developed people skills are not limited to the workplace but extend to every environment where you encounter people. When worked on faithfully and prayerfully, they will enrich all aspects of your professional and personal life. And just as God was pleased that Solomon asked for wisdom, He will be pleased when you ask Him to guide you in your interactions with others. The important thing is to understand that you will only succeed with His help.

POLISH YOUR IMAGE AND NETWORKING SKILLS

Money Mentoring Moment

People will judge you by how you look, speak, and conduct yourself socially. You cannot dismiss this reality as shallow or something that "shouldn't be." You would be wise to invest time and resources in developing a polished image that will advance your goals.

When the emcee completed reading the speaker's impressive bio, she strolled onto the stage in a figure-hugging, leave-nothing-to-the-imagination semiformal dress. The occasion was a Christian women's financial empowerment breakfast. The super sexy, "blinged-out" attire screamed, *Inappropriate!*

In the post-breakfast evaluation meeting later that week, the organizers agreed that her appearance had been a big distraction to what they had hoped would be an inspiring message. They would surely think twice before inviting her back—even though she was nationally known. They agreed that in the future, they would communicate their conservative dress code in the speaker's pre-event information package.

Managing Your Image

I've observed many instances over the past several years in which women speakers, leaders, or other influencers appear to place a higher premium on being sexy than being effective. Cleavage abounds and enhanced buttocks steal the attention. On the other hand, there are those who go to the other extreme and adopt a "Homely Hannah" style, convinced they are scripturally justified in doing so—leaving younger folks to conclude they are probably "old fogies" and out of touch with the times. Homely Hannahs reason that the Lord reprimanded the prophet Samuel for attempting to anoint Eliab (David's oldest brother) to be king of Israel simply because he was tall and handsome: "The LORD said to Samuel, 'Don't judge by his appearance or height, for I have rejected him. The LORD doesn't see things the way you see them. People judge by outward appearance, but the LORD looks at the heart'" (1 Samuel 16:7 NLT). Homely Hannahs and others erroneously conclude that this passage negates, and even pooh-poohs, the importance of our outward appearance. Not so. In fact, we must see this scripture as two powerful but separate truths.

First, we must remember that our outward appearance can indeed influence how people perceive us. I once had a boss who was a brilliant woman, but her beauty routine consisted only of good hygiene. "Lauren" appeared to do absolutely nothing to enhance her appearance. Once, when she was making a presentation to the staff, a male coworker whispered to me, "She obviously hates herself!" I refused to acknowledge his comment. Lauren was more than qualified, technically speaking, for the next level on the organization chart, but the position required someone with a bit more polish and personality to represent the company at various social and political functions. Because she did not fit the bill, she sabotaged her advancement and compensation.

Second, God looks at the heart. Yes, God values character and consecration over clothes or outward appearance. And yes, He is the only one who can look beyond our physical packaging and discern the thoughts and intentions of our hearts. However, this is not a heavenly license to abandon all efforts to be attractive. And, just for the record, no woman is doomed to being unattractive. She just has to be intentional in her pursuit. Being unattractive—like Lauren in the story above—can cost you. You can be personable, confident, energetic, socially polished, and demonstrate good taste in clothes (no matter your size) without being "beautiful" by the world's standards. If you don't have a knack for how to achieve these things, hiring an image consultant or taking a short course at a finishing school will be an investment that will yield a high return.

I enrolled in an extensive training course at the John Robert Powers finishing school immediately upon graduation from college. The instruction in etiquette, wardrobe, makeup, diction, and socializing was a bit pricey, but I'm convinced that the confidence they helped me develop played a significant role in my subsequent promotions and corporate favor. If you can't afford such an investment, hop on the Internet (especially *YouTube.com* for demonstrations) and search for such topics as "how to be an attractive woman," "best fashions for full-figured (or skinny) women," or "etiquette rules."

Whether you are formally trained or self-taught, remember that confidence is rooted in knowledge. Before you know it, you will be like the woman described in Proverbs 31:18: "She perceives that her merchandise is good" (NKJV). When you personally value what you bring to the table, that makes you attractive!

Avoid Image Stealers

As a female on the road to empowerment, you will want to be on guard against these top image busters:

- Being super self-conscious (constantly tugging at your clothes, reapplying lipstick, looking in the mirror, over-emphasizing correct posture, etc.).

- Wearing an outdated hairdo. It's easy to get stuck in a specific decade that you loved with big hair or odd cuts. If I've just described you, it's time to let a stylist show you a few more flattering alternatives.

- Sporting fashions that are ill-fitting or inappropriate for your size. Always aim for a good fit; hire a local tailor to taper your outfits and hemlines to your body.

- Wearing too much makeup or none at all. Consultants who work at makeup counters in departments stores or in cosmetic specialty stores will gladly help you hone your beauty look. Many stores offer free makeovers or will do one for a small fee.

- Not knowing proper dining etiquette. There are tons of books and free articles on this subject so there is no excuse for sitting down at the table and picking up your neighbor's fork (yours is usually on the left), eating her dinner roll (yours on the left), or drinking her water (yours on the right).

- Poor diction and grammar. If in doubt about how to pronounce a word, type it in at *dictionary.com* and listen to the audio feature that pronounces it. This is important. People often draw conclusions about your intellect based on how extensive your vocabulary appears to be and how much command you have of the English language. Build a strong vocabulary by watching or listening to a variety of news talk shows or podcasts and reading high-level newspapers like the *Wall Street Journal*. You can also take advantage of the free online tools and apps to increase your vocabulary (*vocabulary.com*).

Network like a Pro

The woman from the village of Shunem, a place the prophet Elisha frequently passed through, was rich, generous, persuasive, and tenacious; she was also very hospitable. She convinced her husband that they should add a room onto their house to accommodate the prophet's visits. Elisha, ever grateful, wanted to show his appreciation for her kindness.

> "Look, you have been concerned for us with all this care. What can I do for you? Do you want me to speak on your behalf to the king or to the commander of the army?" She answered, "I dwell among my own people" (2 Kings 4:13 NKJV).

The Shunammite's response demonstrated her contentment with her circle of interaction, that is, with her "own people." To some her response may seem humble and laudable, but it was actually naïve and shortsighted. A trap too many women fall into. Elisha was willing to use his influence to connect her with the top echelons of government, but she did not anticipate needing such an association so she dismissed it without further discussion. Over a decade later, she would need exactly what he had offered.

In 2 Kings 8, God called for a seven-year famine in the land. Elisha instructed the woman to relocate to wherever she could until it was over. So she moved to the land of the Philistines. When the famine ended she returned to Shunem, only to find that her property had been taken over by the government. She went to appeal to the king to get it back. Ironically (or providentially), at the time she arrived to see him, Elisha's servant, Gehazi, was already at the palace "shooting the breeze" with him.

> Then the king talked with Gehazi, the servant of the man of God, saying, "Tell me, please, all the great things Elisha has done." Now it happened, as he was telling the king how he had restored the dead to life, that there was the woman whose son he had restored to life, appealing to the king for her house and for her land. And Gehazi said, "My lord, O king, this is the woman, and this is her son whom Elisha restored to life." And when the king asked the woman, she told him.
>
> So the king appointed a certain officer for her, saying, "Restore all that was hers, and all the proceeds of the field from the day that she left the land until now" (verses 4-6 NKJV).

The king didn't hesitate to resolve her problem; she had already been validated by Gehazi—who was validated by Elisha. Ladies, networking is important because God works through people.

It took me a while to embrace this reality. I saw networking as a trap to make me trust in people and their influence rather than in God. So

I resisted it with an "I don't need man; promotion comes from God" attitude. I never tried to curry favor with anybody. I would run the other way from people of influence—even when they showed genuine interest in me.

However, when I saw men who were less qualified than I getting accolades and promotions based on work I had done behind the scenes, the scales fell from my eyes. I finally understood that faith is not a substitute for networking. Further, networking was certainly not about me or what people could do for me. It's about finding ways to add value to other people's lives and helping them reach their goals...and then resting in God's principle of sowing and reaping. I now network regularly, but I don't rest my faith in anybody's ability or willingness to advance my cause. It is God who gives us favor with people for His divine purpose.

If we sow into others, somewhere, somehow we are going to reap the benefit at God's appointed time. So do not rest your faith in networking, but don't neglect it. Monitor your motives so that your goal is never selfish. When you sow favor into others, God will cause people (not always the same folks) to sow into you. I am reminded of several occasions where I have spoken for a charity that did not have the money to pay an honorarium, but I spoke anyway because their cause was worthy. Almost invariably there has been a person in the audience who later used his or her influence to open the door for a paid speaking opportunity.

As I have read the story of the Shunammite again and again, I marvel at how comfortable Gehazi was with having a casual conversation with the king. He was a servant—Elisha's servant. And Elisha wasn't even present! Clearly, he did not possess an "I dwell among my own people" mind-set. Let's take a lesson from men on this one, ladies. We never need to feel unworthy of interacting with powerful folks. This is primarily a female mind-set. In my former thinking, I never would have used a high-ranking dignitary's time as casually as Gehazi did.

I once attended a government-sponsored women's conference held on a popular island nation. Because I was a noted author, they sat me at a VIP table at the event. From the very start, I noticed that the photographers snapped pictures of our table more than all the others. I soon learned that I was sitting next to the president of the country! As the morning progressed, one of the keynote speakers asked us to get into two-person groups. You guessed it. Mr. President selected me as his partner. He shared the personal challenges of his job with me. God gave me just the words to minister to and even caution him on how he was handling his family priorities. He was very encouraged, gave me his cell number, and gave me permission to contact him directly. I never called him. Back then, I was like that Shunammite woman: "I dwell among my own people." Did it even occur to me that with just a nod from him, maybe I could have been one of the speakers at a future conference? Nope! My thinking was, *If God wants me to speak, He'll let the planners know.* Not necessarily!

Look, ladies, we are workers together with God (2 Corinthians 6:1); we have a role to play and actions to take, and so does He. We are responsible for doing our part in the "natural;" He does the "supernatural" on our behalf. What an empowering and profitable partnership!

Once you decide to embrace the concept of networking, here are some practical guidelines to help you put your best foot forward and inspire others to interact with you—or on your behalf.

- Show up. The fact that you may be shy is no reason to shy away from networking opportunities. The only way to overcome a fear is to just do it.

- If name tags are available, they are to be worn on the right, so that when you shake a person's right hand, your eyes naturally stay focused on his right side.

- Hold your glass in your left hand, and keep the right hand dry for handshaking. Hold stemmed glasses by the stem.

- When introducing yourself, say your name slowly (especially if it's difficult to pronounce). Be modest, and do not boast or exaggerate about your experience, background, or well-known acquaintances.

- When introducing others, say the name of the person whom you desire to give the most honor or respect *first*. Social protocols dictate who is more prominent than another. You may simply say, "More Prominent, I'd like to introduce (or "I'd like you to meet") Less Prominent." The guidelines for who is more or less prominent differ in social versus business situations. In social settings, age and gender are the key factors in determining who is to be given the highest honor; however, in the business world, rank and authority determine who has more prominence. Here are a couple of examples:

  Social Introduction: "Bishop Smith, I'd like you to meet my brother, Sam Brown."

  Business Introduction: "President/CEO, I'd like to introduce the new head of the accounting department, Sherry Mason."

- Introduce people to others who you feel would benefit by knowing them. Give each a little bit of information about the other to get the conversational ball rolling.

- Place a supply of business cards in the pocket of your jacket for quick retrieval when someone asks for it. *Do not offer it until asked.* Make sure that the cards are crisp, clean, and free of notes written on the back.

- Follow up immediately on your promise to provide information, product samples, or whatever. Be realistic on the time frame when promising; give yourself a week rather than "tomorrow." Your integrity is at stake. God has promised rewards for those who "keep their promises even when it hurts" (Psalm 15:4 NLT).

When you are comfortable with your appearance and you know the rules of etiquette and social skills, you can be confident in any setting. Remember that confidence is rooted in knowledge—so learn as much as you can. The Internet, your local library, and bookstores are great sources for image-polishing, confidence-building information. My book *Socially Confident in 60 Seconds* is a crash course in social etiquette and networking. Most of the information I have shared in this chapter is discussed in more detail in that book.

ASK FOR WHAT YOU WANT

Money Mentoring Moment

*Ask, and it will be given to you; seek, and you
will find; knock, and it will be opened to you. For
everyone who asks receives, and he who seeks
finds, and to him who knocks it will be opened.*

MATTHEW 7:7-8 NKJV

The things you desire will remain in pending mode until you are courageous enough to ask for them. James 4:2 reminds us, "You do not have because you do not ask God." If you're going to achieve your goals, you must be clear about what you desire and why. Whether it's a raise, a favor, a discount, a promotion, or a concession, make sure whatever you are requesting is for the glory of God. Once you are sure of that, stand on God's promises and trust Him for the outcome.

Responding to "No"

As you become more emboldened to ask for what you want, you will find not every answer will be "yes." However, you must understand that "no" is not always final, and it certainly isn't fatal. When we read the account of the Gentile woman in Matthew 15:23-28 (NKJV) who asked Jesus to come and heal her demon-possessed daughter, the conversation initially sounds out of character for Jesus. However, He was setting her up for a miracle.

But He answered her not a word. *[Totally ignored her. Wow!]*

And His disciples came and urged Him, saying, "Send her away, for she cries out after us." *[Hey, guys, the woman is in distress. Show some compassion!]*

But He answered and said, "I was not sent except to the lost sheep of the house of Israel." *[Jesus, are You really going to discriminate on the basis of her Gentile heritage? We know You came to fulfill the Covenant with the Jews, but come on!]*

Then she came and worshiped Him, saying, "Lord, help me!" *[Hmm, looks like she's not accepting Your "no," Jesus.]*

But He answered and said, "It is not good to take the children's bread and throw it to the little dogs." *[Jesus, we know You didn't insult her. You were trying to make a point that the Jews were Your top priority.]*

And she said, "Yes, Lord, yet even the little dogs eat the crumbs which fall from their master's table." *[Aaahhh, what a comeback. Ignoring the possible humiliation and discrimination, she is still refusing to accept His "no."]*

Then Jesus answered and said to her, "O woman, great is your faith! Let it be to you as you desire." And her daughter was healed from that very hour. *[Yes! Mission accomplished. Well done, Mrs. Gentile! Thanks for your example.]*

Consider embracing the following responses when you are told no:

- Respectfully ask the person why she said no. You may find she did not have all the facts or information or she may have misinterpreted it. At least by asking you can hear directly what the rationale is. Offer empathy for the person's reason and proceed to offer clarity or a rebuttal—if you have a strong, rational one.

- Ask what you must do to get a "yes." If the answer is vague, ask the person to be specific.

- Adopt a divine perspective. You have a desire; God has a

plan. Don't let a "no" drive you into depression or allow it to incapacitate you. Always, always stay at the "nevertheless, not My will, but Yours" point (Luke 22:42 NKJV) regarding all requests. Keep Proverbs 19:21 uppermost in your mind: "You can make many plans, but the LORD's purpose will prevail" (NLT).

- Proceed to Plan B. Always think of alternative ways to achieve the goal. Move forward cautiously, however, lest you lean on your own understanding and make a mess of things. Keep acknowledging God so that He can direct your path.

Asking for a Raise or Promotion

If you are an employee and you have been excellent at your job, you will likely desire a raise or promotion. Knowing what you are worth and asking for what you want are the keys to financial empowerment at work. But it can be difficult to communicate your worth to your boss. Unfortunately, it is rare for a boss to initiate a raise or promotion without any action on your part. Here are some tips to make you more comfortable being the initiator of the request and to minimize the fear of asking:

1. Maintain a log of your accomplishments. I worked at a Fortune 500 company once, and management selected a group of us to fast-track up the corporate ladder. They brought in a psychiatrist to teach us on how to have a success mind-set. He instructed us to maintain a file in which we kept a record of every single accomplishment or action that improved profits or processes, reduced expenses, improved morale, showed our team spirit, or benefited the company in any way. We were to use it as talking points when we asked for a raise or promotion.

2. Ask at the opportune time. If your company is going through budget cuts and layoffs, it might be best to hold

off until things improve. It would be a good idea to ask during your semiannual or annual review, since that is an opportunity set aside for you to discuss your performance with your manager. If you ask and the boss says no, ask him to tell you specifically what you need to do for him to grant your request. Also ask when you can revisit the decision.

3. Know your salary range on the open market. Bring the documentation with you. If you're asking for a raise, be sure to arm yourself with salary statistics. You can research salary information on *Payscale.com* or *Salary.com*. Never, ever ask for a raise because you need it for your household or other personal expenses. Raises are granted based on merit. Show why you merit the desired increase.

If you see after a reasonable time that your request will not be forthcoming, ask God if you should seek greener pastures. Maybe He is trying to tell you something! But no matter what, do not develop a negative attitude. Remain a positive team player until the day you leave. Stay professional in all your responses. This is critical. When it's all said and done, remember that according to Psalm 75:6-7, promotion comes from God. Trust His timing.

Handling Gender Discrimination

Gender discrimination is real. It's not a matter of *if* you will experience it, only *when*. It's still a man's world, though women have certainly come a long way. So when you are faced with discrimination in the workplace, in ministry, or in other areas of life, should you confront it or just leave it in the hands of the Lord? The answer is to respond promptly and peacefully with grace and strength.

The daughters of Zelophehad set a fine example in Numbers 27:1-11. The nation of Israel was on the brink of entering the Promised Land. Each tribe was being assigned their inheritance according to the laws given to Moses by God. However, Zelophehad had died and left no sons. At that time, the law dictated that only men could inherit land. Therefore, Zelophehad's brothers would be the legal heirs of his portion.

Rather than accept this as an unchangeable reality, Zelophehad's five daughters staged a peaceful protest during which they requested what they deserved and desired "Why should the name of our father be removed from among his family because he had no son? Give us a possession among our father's brothers" (verse 4 NKJV). Notice that they acted:

Promptly: They wasted no time in bringing the problem to the attention of Moses and the other leaders. They didn't wait until they arrived in the Promised Land to moan, complain, and have an "ain't it awful" party about how unfair the law was.

Peacefully: They were respectful and peaceful in their approach. They did not demonstrate a negative attitude nor did they give Moses an ultimatum. They simply laid out the situation, asked for what they wanted, and explained why they were entitled to it. When Moses took their case to God, He agreed with them. "The daughters of Zelophehad speak what is right; you shall surely give them a possession of inheritance among their father's brothers, and cause the inheritance of their father to pass to them" (verse 7 NKJV).

Later they showed a willingness to compromise when Moses instructed them that they could indeed inherit their father's land but must marry within their tribe to avoid diluting the inheritance with other tribes (Numbers 36:6).

Because the daughters had the courage to stand up for themselves, they ultimately affected the lives of all women who would find themselves in similar situations in the future. God instituted a new law that if a man died and left no son, his inheritance should be given to his daughters. Mission accomplished!

Being told no could be the beginning, not the end, of your story. Successful people have the confidence and courage to ask for what they want. They do not allow fear to bully them. They know that the only way to fight it is to run toward the battle. Let me reiterate what I said at the beginning of this chapter: "No" is not always final, and it certainly isn't fatal.

LEAD LIKE A WOMAN

Money Mentor Moment

*A woman's intuitiveness, persuasiveness, inclusiveness,
and persistence make her a natural for achieving
personal and professional financial goals.*

love being a woman. Even though we have had an oppressive history and continue to experience many injustices in society worldwide, we are still very high on God's agenda. It's time to get comfortable leading like a woman. And by the way, every woman is a leader. Leadership guru John Maxwell says that leadership is influence—nothing more, nothing less. You do not have to have delegated authority to be a leader; you can simply be one who inspires, motivates, encourages, and influences others. We are all leaders in one environment or another.

Truths That Anchor

Women can face every endeavor with confidence. The following supreme truths are the anchors that assure me I can win and never fail:

1. God set my destiny before I was born. Psalm 139:16 says, "You saw me before I was born. Every day of my life was recorded in your book. Every moment was laid out before

a single day had passed" (NLT). What I'm supposed to be or do has already been determined.

2. Absolutely no one can thwart my purpose. Isaiah 14:27 says, "His hand is stretched out, and who will turn it back?" (NKJV). No woman who embraces this truth ever has to compromise her morals or succumb to depression when advancement opportunities look bleak.

3. When I stay in right standing with Him, He gives me favor with those who can put me at an advantage. Psalm 5:12 says, "You, O LORD, will bless the righteous; with favor You will surround him as with a shield" (NKJV). I don't have to network with the purpose of gaining favor; I just have to show up and allow God to make His moves.

4. He is my Source, my Shepherd, and I shall not lack for anything. He supplies all my needs according to His unlimited resources, and He is not restricted to the channels (jobs, clients, Social Security, etc.) that I normally receive funds through. Philippians 4:19 promises that "God will meet all your needs according to the riches of his glory in Christ Jesus."

5. God has equipped me with the tools I need to succeed in the work He has assigned to my hands. Fear and inadequacy must bow to God's plan. "Sufficiency is from God," says 2 Corinthians 3:5 (NKJV). Musings such as "If only I were prettier, smarter, or more connected, then I could…" have no place in our thought life. We are already adequate for every task. This truth frees us from striving to be perfect, competing, envying, and engaging in other worldly acts in an attempt to shine, to be significant. We are already winners, and each of us has a different destiny.

These truths are so familiar to most of us who have read and maybe even memorized them that they can start to sound trite. We often forget that we are to always apply them to everyday situations. Now, just think of the anxiety we could all avoid if, in the midst of any negative financial or other circumstance, we declared, believed, and acted on these truths.

A Woman's Inherent Traits

God has equipped women with inherent traits that many try to hide or put on the shelf in order to avoid appearing weak or "too much like a woman." I'm going to ask you to reconsider your strategy and embrace the following:

Intuitiveness: Intuition is that inner knowing, perception, or wisdom about a situation without prior study or analysis. This is discernment, a gift from God.

The rich, barren Shunammite woman demonstrated intuition when she perceived that Elisha the prophet was a holy man. Therefore, she didn't hesitate to show extreme hospitality and build an addition to her home to accommodate his visits to the village of Shunem. Out of her association with him came a miracle son, a miracle healing when the son died, and the restoration of her property when the government confiscated it during a famine (2 Kings 4, 8). Her intuition paid off.

Persuasiveness: Remember the story of Abigail, David, and Nabal? Abigail's impassioned plea to David to spare her household (see chapter 4) showed the power of her persuasiveness. She wrapped up her eight-verse monologue (he didn't get a word in until she finished!) by saying, "When the LORD has fulfilled for my lord every good thing he promised concerning him and has appointed him ruler over Israel, my lord will not have on his conscience the staggering burden of needless bloodshed or of having avenged himself" (1 Samuel 25:30-31). David could not resist her persuasiveness. He relented and did not follow through on his threat to annihilate all the men in Nabal's house.

Abigail was not too proud to beg. Because women don't typically have huge egos to protect, we are more likely to ask and even plead for what we want. Don't be reluctant to use your natural persuasiveness or your readiness to ask for help. Being able to persuade other people to embrace your ideas or grant your requests can take you a long way in the workplace and other environments.

Inclusiveness: When I headed the accounting and finance department at a major organization, I made a point of encouraging my staff to develop personal relationships with each other. Decades earlier, this would have been a no-no according to popular management books. I took them out to inexpensive lunches frequently, celebrated everybody's birthday, and shared tips on managing personal finances during our staff meetings. Once when Larry, one of the senior accountants, returned from his family reunion, he confided to the group that he could hardly wait to get back to work because his family had been very contentious and he missed the caring, belonging, and harmony of our group. This knack for forging unity and building teams is a God-given trait that most women have. Corporate America has finally come to appreciate a woman's propensity to build teams versus promoting the competitive "Lone Ranger" mentality.

Persistence: Don't be deterred by circumstances, delays, or discrimination. The woman in Mark 5:25-34 with the issue of blood had already gone broke on ineffective medical treatments and would have continued bleeding for who knows how long had she not pressed through the crowd and touched the hem of Jesus' garment. The widow who begged the insensitive judge for justice would not let up with her appeals. He finally declared, "I don't fear God or care about people, but this woman is driving me crazy. I'm going to see that she gets justice, because she is wearing me out with her constant requests!" (Luke 18:4-5 NLT). Persistence pays off. As women, we usually have "no shame in our game," patience to spare, and a propensity to solve problems. Let's not abandon this quality in order to appear tough "like a man."

Ability to multitask: Deborah was the only woman in the Bible who was mentioned as a judge (Judges 4–5). She ruled Israel at a time when people did their own thing. She had many talents and responsibilities that she handled well. She was a wife, a judge, a motivator, a warrior, a poetess, and a spiritual mother. Further, as a prophetess, she spoke on behalf of God and discerned His purposes. She prophesied victory in a decisive battle with Israel's longtime enemy who had oppressed them for 20 years. The head of the Israeli army insisted on her going into battle with him against such a powerful foe. After the war was won, she composed a song of victory, "The Song of Deborah," that summed up the event (Judges 5). The Israelites then enjoyed peace for over 40 years—under the leadership of a powerful woman. Yes, Judge Deborah was one multitasker. Because most women assume a wide variety of tasks at home, they are already "programmed" to handle lots of duties at once. Of course, we must monitor this natural tendency or we can get too overloaded and burned out.

Obscured Knowledge

You may ask, "How can I avoid being stereotyped as aggressive but still state my desires or preferences in financial and other situations?" First, you must silence the voice in your head that says only men can succeed in the business world. Next, let go of the fear of being judged. You cannot control what others may think. Don't buy into the theory that you have to act masculine to be perceived as strong.

I have found a good strategy is to start asking leading but smart questions to "clarify" (wink) your understanding during discussions. Sure, you may already know the answer to a question, but don't be afraid to open your mouth and let others know you have a brain and it's switched on.

Don't be timid in putting forth your ideas. I have watched women do this in meetings. They often start their input with a statement such as, "I may be wrong, but…" Sometimes they speak at such a low volume, a man often comes right behind them and makes the same suggestion—which others hail as a great idea. Nobody even notices she initiated it. Now, I'm not asking you to yell, but for goodness' sake, say what you have to say with bold certainty. This will convey confidence to others, and you will find people desiring and respecting your input more.

It's not how much you talk but the quality of what you say, so if you tend to be an introvert, use it to your advantage. Wait until you have something to say that adds value; don't just talk for talking's sake, which will surely sabotage your credibility. I know a woman who routinely does this because she wants to have input in the discussion. Therefore, she often comes out of left field with a comment that is totally irrelevant to the matter on the table. Do I need to tell you that she is perceived as an "air head"? I lower my eyes to keep from seeing the confused glances of the other meeting participants.

Leading like a woman is a masterful strategy, so do not shy away from your unique, God-given traits. And make every effort to avoid reinforcing stereotypes about women. Don't be moody, whiny, or unsupportive of other women. Don't sit in the back of the room in organizational meetings—take a prominent seat. You belong; act like it. Know your stuff, but don't become obsessive about trying to know a lot about everything. There is a difference between excellence and neurotic perfection.

Part 4

SHARPEN
YOUR SAW

14

UNDERSTAND FINANCIAL TERMINOLOGY

Money Mentoring Moment

In the financial world, one must be able to speak the language—or blindly trust those who do, thereby subjecting themselves to their interpretations and control.

Are you ready to learn how to talk the talk of finances? Following is a crash course in the terminology and jargon used in common financial transactions. Next time you hear these terms used you will have a working understanding of what they mean and can ask relevant questions about them if necessary.

Debt, Borrowing, and Credit Transactions

Debtor: A person or entity that owes money to another party.

Creditor: A person, bank, or other enterprise that lends money or extends credit to another party.

Principal: The initial amount of the loan or the outstanding balance—excluding any unpaid interest.

Interest: The cost of borrowing; always expressed in terms of an *annual* percentage rate. To determine the monthly rate, simply divide it by 12. The interest portion of a loan payment is computed as follows: outstanding principal balance times monthly interest rate times the number of days in the month. Example: X Bank made you a $200,000 loan at 6 percent for 30 years. Your monthly interest rate will be .5 percent (6 percent divided by 12 months) or .005.

Term: The amount of time (months or years) the loan will be outstanding before it is due. In home mortgages, the normal term is 30 years (360 months); but you can also apply for 10-, 15-, and 20-year loans. The longer the *term*, the lower the monthly payment will be and the more interest you will pay—since you are taking longer to pay off the debt. The shorter the term, the higher the monthly payment—since you are paying the debt off faster. A smart move, if you are financially disciplined and your cash flow allows, is to contract for a longer loan *term* and then make extra payments when you can so that you pay the loan off earlier, and save on the interest expense. If you run into difficult times, you can always resume the lower contractual payment.

Amortization Period: Don't let this big word scare you! It simply means the number of months or years used to *compute* the monthly payment on your loan. In most instances of home and car loans, the *amortization period* and the *term* will be the same number of years—but they do not have to be. For example, a lender may offer a 15-year (180 months) loan *term* with a 30-year *amortization* period. This means that your monthly payment is computed assuming it will take you 30 years (360 months) to pay off the loan, but whatever the outstanding balance is at the end of 180 months must be paid in full—via a balloon payment (see definition below). You will then need to pay off the loan or refinance it at the end of the term. Now, if the loan term and the amortization period are the same, then the loan will be fully amortized (paid off) at the end of the loan term.

Amortization also refers to the process of paying off a loan through regular payments over a period of time. A portion of each payment is first applied to interest while the remaining amount is used to amortize or pay down the principal amount.

Points: In connection with a mortgage, a point is equal to one percent of the loan amount and refers to the loan fees charged by the lender for originating the loan. Two points (2%) on a $100,000 loan would be $2,000.

Balloon Payment: This is a lump sum payable at the end of a loan *term.* Balloon payments occur when the *amortization period* is longer than the loan *term.* For example, if the loan term is 10 years but the monthly payment is computed based on 20 years (a 20-year amortization period), you will have a lump sum due at the end of 10 years because the payments have been too low to pay off or "fully amortize" the loan.

Forbearance: A period of time (months, quarters, or similar periods) during which the lender halts or reduces the payments on a loan due to a borrower's financial hardship. Although the payments are suspended, the interest continues to be charged (accrued) and is added to the outstanding loan balance.

Escrow: A legal concept in which a third party holds assets or agreements in their care until both parties meet the conditions of the transaction.

Impound Account: (This has nothing to do with dogs!) This is an account set up and maintained by a lender to collect property taxes, hazard insurance, private mortgage insurance, and other payments from borrowers who put down less than 20 percent of the purchase price. Lenders consider low-down-payment borrowers a higher risk since they have less "skin in the game." Impound amounts are computed separately from the principal and interest payment but are remitted by the borrower with the regular payment. Make no bones about it, the primary purpose of the impound account is to protect the lender, but it also helps borrowers manage their cash flow better by not having to come up with a lump sum at certain times of the year when the underlying expense (taxes, insurance, etc.) payments are due.

Loan to Value Ratio (LTV): A calculation that measures the relationship between the loan amount and the value of the related collateral (house, car, etc.). If a lender extends a $70,000 loan against a property with a market value of $100,000, the Loan to Value Ratio is 70 percent ($70,000/$100,000). This means that there is a 30 percent cushion just in case the collateral must be sold to repay the loan. In conventional mortgage financing, the lenders will typically lend up to 90 percent of the value of a residence. LTV is even lower for investment properties, as they carry more risk. A deal is more attractive to a lender if the borrower has more equity in the property—which would cause her to be less likely to walk away. For example, if the borrower defaults on the $70,000 loan above, the lender can sell the $100,000 asset at a discount and still fully recover the amount of the loan. Now, if the lender had financed 100 percent of a sale (it has happened!) and the borrower defaults on the $100,000 loan, the lender will have to pay for commissions, repairs, or other costs to sell the asset and will most likely incur a loss on the transaction.

Mortgage Broker: An independent, federally licensed agent or company who manages the process of getting you a mortgage. She applies on your behalf with various lenders, finds the best rates, negotiates terms, and helps you get approved. She is paid a commission (around one percent [1%] of the mortgage amount) for her services, which is often included in "loan origination fees." In some instances, the cost of the mortgage broker is reflected in a higher interest rate that you pay for over the course of the loan; this is expensive. However, she will save you a lot of time and frustration, as the whole loan underwriting process can test the patience of most of us. Besides, some lenders only work with mortgage brokers, so without one, you may be shut out of access to better terms. But if you don't mind the hassle or have a great banking relationship with an existing lender, then work with the institution's loan officer directly—and save some money.

Private Mortgage Insurance (PMI): This is insurance charged by a conventional mortgage lender when a borrower pays less than 20 percent down on a home. It protects the lender from losing money if the borrower defaults. PMI is also required if a borrower *refinances* the mortgage with less than 20 percent equity in the property. Once your equity (property market value minus the loan balance) in the property exceeds 20 percent, you may petition the lender to drop the insurance.

Negative Amortization: This occurs when the amount of a loan payment is not sufficient to cover the interest charges for the period. The deficient amount gets *added* to the outstanding balance of the loan. Example: If the loan payment is $1,000 but the interest expense alone (because of rising interest rates) is $1,100, then $100 will be added to the loan balance. The borrower literally ends up owing more than the initial loan. This usually occurs in an adjustable rate mortgage or with student loans. This is also referred to as "NegAm."

Reverse Mortgage: This is a type of home loan that allows homeowners over 62 years of age to borrow against their home equity and to put off repayment of the loan until they sell, move out of the home, or pass away. Borrowers remain responsible for property taxes and homeowner's insurance. *Because there are no required mortgage payments, the interest due* is added to the loan balance each month. The increasing loan balance can eventually grow to exceed the value of the home. In the event of the borrower's death, the heirs are not required to repay any deficit amount if the proceeds from the sale of the home are not sufficient to pay off the loan. The lender simply repossesses the house.

Joint Tenancy with Right of Survivorship: When you purchase real estate with another person, you have options on how you can hold title. If you chose to hold title as joint tenants, both of the owners share title *equally*. When one owner dies, the survivor receives the deceased's share automatically. This "survivor takes all" option cannot be overwritten by the deceased person's will. Property held in joint tenancy does not have to go through the probate process. Most married couples choose this option. However, it has a key disadvantage—especially for unmarried or unrelated owners. Each owner can be sued by a creditor for up to her share. This presents a risk in that the property may have to be sold to satisfy the creditor. So think twice about putting your adult child or other persons on your deed simply to avoid probate. Your attorney will most likely recommend putting the property in a living trust.

Tenants in Common: Some owners, especially if they are not married to each other, choose to hold title to their property as Tenants in Common. In this case, the owners can specify in the deed what percentage of the property each owns (40/60, 80/20, etc.) The ownership does not have to be equal as in the case of Joint Tenants. The major advantage of this option is that each owner can will her portion to whomever she desires. This may prove to be a good option for some second marriages since the spouses can will their individual portions to their children from a previous marriage. A major disadvantage is that when an owner dies, her share has to go through the cost and delays of a probate court process. The remaining co-owner could end up sharing title with someone she doesn't know or like.

Chapter 13 (individuals only) Bankruptcy: A filing by an individual that puts her on a three- to five-year payment plan to pay off her debts and keep her property.

Chapter 7 (individuals) Bankruptcy: This is the most common type of bankruptcy filing for individuals who can no longer pay their bills. It allows you to wipe out qualifying debt while keeping the things that you'll need to live and work. Property that is exempt from sale varies from state to state. Generally, debtors are allowed to keep their home, car, and personal belongings. While this legal procedure allows debt to be dismissed, it severely damages credit. Future credit will be expensive to obtain, if at all. But not so fast! You have to meet stringent criteria before you can qualify for this filing. The law also requires that eight years must pass before you can file again.

Chapter 7 (business) Bankruptcy: A filing in which a company ceases operations and closes its doors. The court appoints a trustee to sell the company's assets, the proceeds are used to pay off the debts, and then the remaining debt is written off.

Chapter 11 (business only) Bankruptcy: A form of bankruptcy that is filed by businesses to allow them to reorganize their affairs and restructure debts under an approved plan while they keep operating without worrying about creditors forcing them into a *Chapter 7* liquidation of the business.

Retirement/Investing

Traditional IRA (Individual Retirement Account): The Internal Revenue Service (IRS) allows an individual to contribute a portion of her earned income (before it is taxed) toward retirement. There is an annual limit on the amount of income you can make (as a single or married person) to qualify for the IRA deduction. The IRS also limits the amount of the annual IRA contribution. As of 2018, the maximum contribution is $5,500 and is not available to singles who earn more than $63,000, and couples earning more than $101,000. People over 50 can contribute an extra $1,000. Every year the IRS announces updated contribution limits and earned income thresholds. Since the limits are always changing, you can simply go to *IRS.gov* and type in "Traditional IRA limits" to get the current year's amounts.

The investment is made on a pre-tax basis, meaning it can be deducted from the current year's income. You will not have to pay taxes on the income or the earnings from the investments until you withdraw the money. If you withdraw any funds before you reach age 59½, you must include the withdrawal in your regular income and be taxed at regular income tax rates on it. (There are certain circumstances where they will make an exception.) You will also be assessed a ten percent early withdrawal penalty. The penalty is not assessed if you wait until after you reach 59½; however, you must still include the withdrawal in your regular income and be taxed on it at regular rates. In the year that you reach 70½, you can no longer make contributions. Further, you must start withdrawing a minimum amount based on an IRS formula that works out to about 4 percent per year. At that rate, it would take about 25 years to deplete the account and you'd be about ready to retire to heaven at the ripe age of approximately 95. The withdrawals will always be taxable.

Roth IRA: This account is different from the traditional IRA in several ways. Your retirement contributions are made with *after-tax* dollars. This means you do not get a deduction when you make contributions to the account. You pay taxes currently on the earned income that you made during the year. The good news is that withdrawals from the account, including the investment earnings, are tax-free. That's right—tax-free. And there are more pluses here. There are no penalties for taking the money out once you've had the account for at least five years. You may withdraw your contributions to a Roth IRA penalty-free at any time for any reason, but you'll be penalized for withdrawing any *investment earnings before age 59½,* unless it's for a "qualifying reason." (Go to *irs.gov* to learn what they are.) Some people convert their traditional IRA into a Roth IRA and pay the penalty for doing so, as all of the converted amount must be taxed. It's still advantageous to do this because the earnings from then on from the new Roth IRA will not be taxed when the funds are eventually withdrawn. Converted funds cannot be taken out penalty-free until at least five years after the conversion. With a Roth IRA, you are not required to start making withdrawals at age 70½; you can leave the money in for as long as you want, allowing it to grow as you get older.

There is an annual limit on the amount of *income* you can earn (as a single or married person) to qualify to participate in the Roth IRA as well as the *contribution* amount. It's a bit more complicated, but basically the earned income limits are higher than for the traditional IRA. In 2018, if you are single and your MAGI (Modified Adjusted Gross Income) exceeds $135,000, you cannot contribute to a Roth IRA; the MAGI maximum for married filers is $199,000.

401(k) and 403(b): These are retirement plans offered by for-profit companies and tax-exempt entities, respectively. These plans are both tax-advantaged. Employee contributions are made on a pretax basis and the earnings grow tax-free. The plans are subject to IRS employee contribution limits. The contributions limit for 2018 is $18,500, with employees over 50 years old getting an extra $6,500 "catch up" allowance for a total employee contribution of $25,000. As a general rule, you will incur a ten percent penalty tax in addition to regular income taxes if you take a distribution from your 401(k) or 403(b) prior to age 59½.

Capital Gain: This is the increase in the value of a capital asset over the original cost. A capital gain may be short-term (one year or less) or long-term (more than one year). Capital gain is also the profit that an individual makes when she sells a fixed or capital asset such as stocks and land or buildings, a vehicle, and so forth for more than it cost; the cost will include all expenditures made since the purchase that improved the life of the asset. If you pay $200,000 for an asset and five years later it is worth $250,000, you have a $50,000 capital gain.

Capital Loss: The decrease in a capital asset's market value compared to its purchase price plus improvements (if any) made to it since it was purchased.

Realized Capital Gains and Losses: These occur when an asset is sold. This triggers a taxable event. Unrealized gains and losses, sometimes referred to as "paper" gains and losses, means that you haven't actually sold the asset but if you were to, this would be the gain or loss amount. Gains or losses are not claimed for tax purposes until they are "realized."

Dividend: The distribution of a portion of a corporation's profits to the stockholders. A corporation has two options on what it can do with its earnings: distribute a portion, or retain all or a portion and use the funds to grow the business.

Estate Planning

Will: A legal document that sets forth instructions on how a person wishes his possessions to be distributed after he dies. It can be formally prepared or handwritten ("Holographic Will").

Term Life Insurance: Insurance for a specific number of years. See additional discussion in chapter 20, "Deal with the Unexpected."

Whole Life Insurance: A policy in force during the entire life of the insured as long as the premiums are current.

Living Trust: See discussion in chapter 20, "Deal with the Unexpected."

Life Estate: A type of estate that only lasts for the lifetime of the beneficiary. A life estate prevents the beneficiary from selling the property or willing it to his heirs. Example: Hannah and Joseph, both over 65, married in 2017. Joseph owned his own home, which he wanted to leave to his adult children. Not wanting to put Hannah at a disadvantage should he die first, he signed a Life Estate agreement that lets Hannah occupy the property as long as she is alive and resides there. At her death, the title of the property can then be transferred to Joseph's designated heirs.

Estate: Everything of value that a person owns no matter how little or how much. It includes real estate, investments, cash value of whole life insurance policies, art collections, antiques, and any other assets—minus any outstanding loans against them. Yup, you can have a $100 estate if that's all you own.

Executor: The person responsible for managing the affairs of a deceased person's probate estate.

Probate: The court process in which the court determines if a will is valid and authorizes the executor to distribute the assets of the deceased person.

Payable on Death (POD) Account: An account in which the owner has named a specific beneficiary to receive the funds in the account when the owner dies. POD accounts are not subject to the probate process; the beneficiary simply presents a copy of the death certificate and appropriate identification to the financial institution to obtain the funds.

Accounting/Financial Statements

Assets: Anything that is owned and will provide future benefit. Assets can be (1) "current"—expected to be used up (supplies) or converted to cash (Accounts Receivable) within the next 12 months of the Balance Sheet date, or (2) "noncurrent"—providing value beyond one year (vehicles, real estate, and the like). See chapter 2 "Determine Where You Stand" for a listing of Asset categories.

Liabilities: Any amount owed to another. Could be short-term (due within the next 12 months [e.g., accounts payable]) or long-term (due after one year [e.g., a mortgage]).

Income Statement: A financial statement that lists income/revenues minus the expenses over a certain period (month, quarter, year). The difference between income and expenses is called net income or net loss.

Depreciation: The write-off of a fixed asset over its economic life. For example, a vehicle may be written off or depreciated for tax purposes over five years. If it cost $50,000, the annual depreciation expense (write-off) will be $10,000. The Internal Revenue Service has guidelines for the number of years that particular assets can be depreciated over. Depreciation expense is tax deductible even though it is a "paper" expense instead of a cash expenditure. This is a great tax break for people who own fixed assets.

This is just a brief summary of the terms you will want to be familiar with. To continue to increase your financial vocabulary, consider signing up for the daily definitions sent out by *Investopedia.com*.

15

EMBRACE TECHNOLOGY

Money Mentoring Moment

We live in an information age, and those who are wise will learn how to access key information quickly as well as how to disseminate it to the masses via the Internet and social media.

When undertaking any endeavor, having the right tools can make all the difference. In this age of technology, a variety of tools are available to assist in every area of your finances. Following are some tips to help you become a savvy woman who uses her computer, smartphone, or tablet for her advantage and empowerment.

Financial Management Tools

It's never been easier to manage your personal and business finances. Whether you need help budgeting, saving, paying off debt, or investing, software applications are available to help you be more efficient. Here are a few examples of the available tools:

QuickBooks.com: Allows you to manage bills, track mileage, track income and expenses, and manage invoicing and payments. It is an excellent, user-friendly tool for personal and business use.

Mint.com: A free app created by the makers of QuickBooks that allows you to create a budget, track spending, connect bank accounts and credit cards, and pay bills. Mint also offers a free credit score and can be set up to send reminders when a bill is due.

Acorns.com: An app that helps you save money automatically. Connect a card to the app, and it will round each purchase up to the nearest dollar amount and invest the difference in the exchange-traded fund of your choice. The cost is $1 per month.

YouNeedABudget.com: This app forces you to live within your income by allocating a destination for each dollar. The tool offers a built-in accountability partner and provides online classes that teach budgeting basics. There is a small annual fee for its use.

Wally.me: A free app that helps track expenses and allows you to take pictures of receipts instead of manually logging that data. It can capture the amount of each expenditure as well as the location where the item was purchased.

Making Wise Purchasing Decisions

An important aspect of enhancing your financial health is making wise purchasing decisions. Here are some ways you can use technology to save money when shopping:

Comparison Shopping: Suppose you want to purchase an iPad Pro and need to find the best price. Visit *Google.com* and type in the search bar "best price for iPad Pro." A list of various retailers and their prices will appear. At the time of this writing, Walmart had the best deal. However, be aware that the first, top-of-the-list vendors that appear are sponsored results, meaning the retailers paid Google to be shown in that spot.

Using Amazon: Amazon is a giant when it comes to selling products. From dog food to appliances, Amazon likely has whatever you're searching for, and often at the right price. Further, you can save additional time and money with Amazon Prime, a yearly subscription service that provides free two-day shipping. The subscription also includes other perks such as member-only discounts and access to free music, movies, TV shows, and books.

Cable TV Alternative: By 2020, the average cable bill is expected to increase to around $140 per month. And if you consider typical cable add-ons, the monthly payment could be even more. When money is tight, the luxury of cable is often the first candidate for the cutting board. In recent years, with the rise of streaming services, people have been limiting their cable subscriptions or canceling their services altogether. Popular streaming services include Netflix, Hulu, and Amazon Prime. The cost runs anywhere from $10 to $12 a month. And for those who really need specialty channels like HBO and Starz, Hulu and Amazon offer separate subscriptions to these services, which is still a significant reduction in cost compared to cable. To take advantage of streaming services, all you need is your computer, tablet, or smartphone. You can now take advantage of even more advanced technology with a smart TV, which has all the most popular streaming apps built in. There are also devices you can attach to your TV, such as Roku or Apple TV, to access more viewing options.

Couponing Sites: Let us not forget coupons, which is how many women save money. Coupons remain a great way to cut corners, but it's no longer necessary to cut them out of newspapers, unless you want to. Here are just a few of the popular coupon/savings sites:

1. *eBates.com*
2. *Coupons.com*
3. *RetailMeNot.com*
4. *RedPlum.com*
5. *SmartSource.com*
6. *ShopAtHome.com*
7. *Savings.com*
8. *SlickDeals.com*

9. *TheKrazyCouponLady.com*

10. *Groupon.com*

Business Productivity and Marketing

In the past, entrepreneurs needed substantial capital to compete with other businesses or they wouldn't last. Today, technology gives everyone the opportunity to hang their shingle and compete on equal footing.

Facebook. By now, almost everyone has a Facebook account. It's handy for keeping track of family and friends, getting the daily news, finding long-lost loved ones, and even just for entertainment. But Facebook really shines when it comes to helping businesses. Entrepreneurs and small businesses can set up a Facebook page, which offers many benefits, the biggest of which is a platform to reach your followers about your products or services. The page is free, but only to a point. For wider reach and greater impact, advertising is the way to go. Rates start as low as $5 to reach thousands of potential customers.

The old-school way of advertising was to take out print ads in magazines or newspapers or create television and radio ads. These advertising venues are expensive. But Facebook allows businesses to run inexpensive ads that target their desired market. For example, let's say you specialize in making antique cat jewelry. Facebook allows you to set up an ad that will target only people who like cats, antiques, and jewelry. And if necessary, you could further limit the audience by age and location.

Cloud Storage. This technology is a crucial tool for many businesses because of the peace of mind it provides. Cloud storage is used to back up personal and business files, as well as entire networks. It is also used as a convenience to allow access to files on the go. Suppose you have a laptop at home, a tablet you carry with you, and a computer in your office at work. In the old days, you would have had to put your files on some type of removable media like a floppy disk or USB drive and take it with you to access the required files. Today this is no longer necessary. Now you can save your files to the cloud storage provider of your choice, sign in on any computer, tablet, or phone, and gain immediate access to any of your files.

Two of the most popular cloud storage providers are *Dropbox .com* and Google Drive. Both provide a certain amount of free space, with paid tiers available depending on how much space you require. Microsoft is another provider. Their subscription model, Microsoft 365, comes with OneDrive, which is their unlimited cloud storage system. Their monthly plan is currently under $10 per month.

Website Development. Every entrepreneur needs a website with a professional domain name. *WordPress.org* is one of the best ways to accomplish this, providing all of the tools you need for free. The site offers a variety of templates to easily build a blog or website. You can even change them periodically for a fresh look, all with the click of a button. Plugins (software that can be added to the site to enhance its functions) are available for everything from social media sharing buttons to newsletter signup boxes. (Make sure you use *WordPress .org* rather than *WordPress.com*, as the .com has limited functionality.)

You will also need a hosting company to host the WordPress installation. Web hosting is a service that allows organizations and individuals to post a website or web page onto the Internet. A web host, or web hosting service provider, is a business that provides the technologies and services needed for the website or webpage to be viewed on the Internet. Websites are hosted, or stored, on special computers called servers.

When Internet users want to view your website, all they need to do is type your website address or domain into their browser. Their computer will then connect to your server, and your webpages will be delivered to them through the browser. The process may sound difficult, but it is really quite simple to set up. If this is too much for you, hire someone to set it up for you. This is why you establish a working capital reserve so that you can afford to hire folks to perform such services.

E-mail Service Providers. At some point you may want to start a newsletter and build a list of subscribers to market your products or to send out inspirational messages, or just to stay connected. To do this, you need a special e-mail service provider, as it is actually against the law to use your private e-mail to send bulk e-mails to a list. You need a way for people to opt in and opt out, and a way to legally capture their information. E-mail services typically charge by the number of subscribers, and once you get into the tens of thousands, it can get pretty pricey. MailChimp (*mailchimp.com*) and MailerLite (*mailerlite.com*) are both free entry-level options for those just getting started. MailChimp is free up to 2,000 subscribers, and MailerLite is free up to 1,000. Even though MailerLite offers fewer subscribers in their free option, their paid plans are cheaper overall. For larger lists, check out *Robly.com*, *Constant Contact.com*, and others. You can compare prices and services with a simple Google search.

Online Freelancers. Big businesses have hundreds of employees to divide the work and keep everything running smoothly. Entrepreneurs and small businesses often have only one or two people to do the work, and one of them is usually the owner. Again, technology has come to the rescue. Entrepreneurs don't have to rent an office building and fill it with employees they can't afford; rather, they can simply hire freelancers to complete work for them. Many websites exist to help entrepreneurs hire the help they need, in whatever field desired. On *Upwork.com*, one can find a website designer, typesetter, ghostwriter, editor, book cover designer, data entry clerk, or a general virtual assistant. These services are also available on *Fiverr .com*, where people perform various services in $5 increments. Some people view Fiverr as a subpar site because of the low initial cost of some gigs (jobs). It's true you get what you pay for, but many people who cannot afford to spend much money have satisfactorily used the site. I've successfully used them for CD cover designs when I wanted to test the waters. Sites that focus solely on hiring virtual assistants also exist, such as *FancyHands.com*.

Videos/Online Courses/Other. Perhaps you aren't ready to use free-lancers just yet, but you aren't equipped to do everything that needs to be done. That's where technology can help. A wealth of information is available on the Internet about how to do just about anything. The top search engine to use for hands-on learning is *YouTube.com*. Simply visit the site and type in a question or phrase. YouTube will return several video results demonstrating step-by-step how to implement the task. If you want to learn something in more detail and have money to spend, you can take a course from places such as *Udemy.com*, *Skillshare.com*, and *Lynda.com*.

Many women are uncomfortable or intimidated by technology, but you don't have to be. Ecclesiastes 10:10 states, "If the ax is dull and its edge unsharpened, more strength is needed, but skill will bring success." With so much information available, there is really no reason not to embrace technology to assist you in becoming financially empowered. Since technology is ever evolving, some of the information presented here may soon be outdated; but once you become adept at searching on the Internet, you can always find the updated data.

One of the wisest things you can do as a woman is pass on these skills to your daughters and equip them for dealing with the technological world we now live in. Encourage them to major in STEM (science, technology, engineering, and mathematics) fields, as they lead to better jobs that can give them a head start to dreaming big and achieving their goals.

PURCHASE BIG-TICKET ITEMS LIKE A PRO

Money Mentoring Moment

*Purchasing "like a pro" is about gaining a working
knowledge of the terminology, negotiable terms,
and pitfalls surrounding big-ticket items.*

Learning to purchase big-ticket items without losing your shirt is a skill every woman must develop. Some of the knowledge you need can be obtained from the Internet, which goes back to the importance of embracing technology (discussed in chapter 15).

Buying a Home

Buying a home will probably be the single largest purchase the average woman will make during her lifetime. Since the most complicated hurdle in buying a home is finding and negotiating a mortgage, that's what we will focus our discussion on here. See chapter 14, "Understanding Financial Terminology," for additional explanations of financial terms and loan jargon used below.

When it comes to mortgages, there are three main types: conventional, FHA, and VA loans.[1]

Conventional loans are best for those with good or excellent credit. They are standard loans with conservative approval guidelines, which include credit scores, a minimum down payment, and a debt-to-income ratio. The amount due at closing can be substantial when considering the down payment, various fees, and mortgage insurance. The FICO (Fair Isaac Corporation) credit score is the most widely used metric in lending decisions and ranges from 300 to 850. A score of 750 to 850 is considered excellent, and those with a score in that range have access to the lowest rates and best loan terms.

FHA loans are administered by the Federal Housing Administration. These loans are more flexible, catering to those who have low credit scores, who can only make small down payments, and whose monthly mortgage will be a significant portion of their take-home pay. The FHA doesn't actually lend money but rather insures the mortgages made by the selected lending institutions. The down payment requirement can be as low as 3.5 percent, and people can qualify with credit scores as low as 580. The disadvantage of FHA loans are the required insurance premiums, which can only be eliminated if you refinance.

VA loans are administered by the Veterans Administration for current and prior members of the armed services. Often no down payment is required for qualified buyers, but they may be required to pay closing costs, as the seller is not required to do so. An earnest deposit may also be required. A VA loan doesn't require mortgage insurance. The VA doesn't lend money but guarantees loans made by private lenders. VA loans are attractive because the borrower can qualify for 100 percent financing. In addition, veterans can use their VA benefits to purchase a home more than once.

There are some limitations in obtaining a VA loan.[2] For example, the VA is only willing to assume a certain amount of liability. So even though there is no limit on how much you can borrow, the VA limits how much you can borrow before you have to make a down payment. In addition, the VA has stricter requirements on the condition of the home you purchase; it must sufficiently pass their inspection guidelines. The VA doesn't have a minimum credit score requirement, but many lenders require a score of at least 620.

Mortgage Pitfalls to Avoid

Don't get locked into an undesirable contract. When you purchase a home, there will be a substantial amount of paperwork to sign. The standard contracts may seem nonnegotiable, but they aren't. Don't feel like you have to sign any contract "as is." Take time to review the paperwork carefully and ask for revisions if necessary. If you don't feel comfortable with such negotiations, a Realtor can help.

Buy what you can afford. The loan amount you are approved for and the loan amount you can afford may be very different. Your income may look good on paper, enough to be approved for a large amount, but realistically it may be beyond your budget. A good rule of thumb is to make sure your mortgage-related expenses are no more than 35 to 40 percent of your gross income—depending on the state where you reside. This includes the mortgage, insurance, homeowner's association fees (if applicable), and real estate taxes, all of which can quickly add up. And don't forget maintenance. The luxury of the responsible landlord handling such problems will be no more.

Buy with the future in mind. Buying a home is a long-term commitment, often 20 years or more. During that time you will experience many changes. Consider your long-term goals. If you are planning to change jobs, retire, have kids, or get married, you'll want to make sure that the house you purchase now will still be affordable and meet your needs later. If you plan to move in a couple of years, buying a house may not be a good idea because if you turn around and sell it after only two years, it will cost you approximately eight percent of the selling price for the sales commission and other fees. Thus, the house you buy would need to increase in value by at least eight percent (four percent per year for two years) just to break even. There is a good chance that the area where you buy the home may not be experiencing that rate of increase in prices.

Beware of fixer-uppers. You may find a home that has great possibilities but needs to be fixed up a bit. It is critical to get a good estimate of the cost of all the repairs and improvements you might want to make. Paint, wallpaper, and carpet may not be too expensive, but state-of-the-art appliances and the cost for remodeling cabinets and counters can add up quickly. Engage the services of a reputable construction professional to help you get a scope on the total cost of all planned expenditures. Make a schedule of when you plan to make the expenditures so that you can match your cash flow and avoid becoming "house rich" but "cash poor."

Don't rush the decision. Home ownership may be the American Dream, but haste can quickly turn it into the American Nightmare. Many times when a woman reaches a certain age and sees everyone around her purchasing homes, she feels she should be doing the same. Do your homework and make a rational decision rather than one based on emotions.

Holding Title

(Please see chapter 14 for a brief discussion on Joint Tenancy vs. Tenants in Common.)

Buying a Vehicle

It's highly likely that you may need to purchase a new or replacement car in the near future. But there are many ways to get ripped off when purchasing a car, so here are ten steps to help you through the process.

1. Do your research. Gone are the days when you had to go from car lot to car lot to shop and apply for a car loan. Now you can do much of your homework online to save both time and money. *ConsumerFinance.gov* has great educational information to help you learn about purchasing a car. Another great site is *Edmunds.com*. Here you can find out how much the car you want really should cost. From there, you can visit various car dealer sites online to determine whether they have the car you want at the price you desire. Often you can fill out a credit application on their sites as well.

2. Get your paperwork in order. To begin the process, you will need to gather important paperwork such as proof of

your employment and salary, the balances on your debt, and if you are self-employed, the last two to three years of your income tax returns.

3. Get preapproved for a loan. It can be really disappointing to get excited about a car only to find out you cannot meet the lender's qualifying criteria. Do your homework online by using a financial calculator (*financialcalculator.org*) to predetermine what your loan payment will be at various price levels based on your trade-in and down payment. Preapproval is the secret to a successful vehicle negotiation. Go to your bank or credit union and find out the amount and interest rate you are approved for. Then you can go to the car dealership armed with the knowledge of the budget available to you to see how rates and terms compare to financing offered by the dealer. Actually, the manufacturer is offering the financing; the dealer is simply processing the loan.

4. Align the vehicle cost with your budget. Ideally, you should plan to spend no more than 15 percent of your gross income on transportation, including gasoline, insurance, maintenance and repairs, annual registration, and so forth. This category can fluctuate widely depending on what part of the country you reside. In Southern California, where a car is almost an absolute necessity, the costs will be significantly higher.

5. Set a maximum financing period. The best car loan terms are those that are no longer than 60 months with a ten percent down payment. Don't be sucked into thinking you are getting a good deal because the dealer is willing to reduce your payments by giving you a longer loan term. Do the math. Use a simple calculator to multiply the proposed monthly payment times the number of payments; this is the absolute amount that you will be paying for your vehicle. Terms longer than five years may

put you at risk of owing more on the car than it is worth after several years.

6. Assess the value of your trade-in. Use *Edmunds.com* to get a handle on the value of your trade-in if you have one. Doing this before visiting the dealership will help you determine whether they are offering you a good deal. Edmunds will provide the following information for your old car: the trade amount the dealer may offer, the trade amount a private buyer may offer, and the price the dealer may retail the car for. Another option is to use *Carmax.com*. They will appraise your car and make you an offer. You are not obligated to sell your car to them or buy a car from them. In fact, you can then use their offer to negotiate with another car dealership.

7. Determine what a good car deal is to you. After you have done your research, you should have a good idea of what a good car deal would look like for you. This takes into consideration the make and model of the car, the price, the interest rate, the loan term, and special accessories. Take the time to find the car that will make you happy and that you feel has the best price and terms available. Be honest about why you desire a particular car. Be sure you are not buying prestige or self-esteem.

8. Test drive like a pro. Don't get so excited about purchasing the car that you don't check the basics, like tires, preferred accessories, room for a car seat, cargo space, etc. Some salespeople prefer to ride with you during the test drive and will only take you around the block. Don't be afraid to take a longer drive. After all, you will be stuck with the car for the next few years, so be sure it's the one you want.

9. Don't give in to pressure. Car salespersons are notorious for their high-pressure tactics to convince you to purchase the car immediately. If you know you are prone to giving in

to pressure, take a male friend whose job will be to frown and tell you to sleep on it. If you need a couple of days to decide, do so! If you're worried the car may not be there later, you can often leave a small deposit to ensure the dealer doesn't sell the car before you've made your decision.

10. Review the contract. By the time the contract is drawn up, you've likely already discussed the pertinent details. However, that doesn't mean you should just skim the contract and sign on the dotted line. Most vehicle purchase contracts are uniform, but you should still take your time and review every line and every word. Unfortunately, sometimes dealerships sneak in extras that seem nonnegotiable. But remember that everything is negotiable; you just need the courage to ask for changes when necessary.

11. Don't be afraid to walk away—even at the last minute. Until you sign a contract, you are not under any obligation to make a purchase. If any of the details are disagreeable to you and you can't work out the terms with the dealership, indicate you are no longer interested and leave. This can be difficult to do if you really want a car, but it's necessary to have the mind-set that you can and will walk away. "Annette" was recovering from bad credit and found a dealership that would work with her to purchase a brand-new car with no down payment. But when she arrived, they tried to change the terms. She called off the deal and left the dealership. The next day a salesman showed up at her house, in the car she had desired to purchase, and said, "Let's do this on your terms." It may seem that car dealerships have the upper hand, but they really don't. You have all the power because only you have the ability to say yes or no. You are not trying to "win friends and influence people" here; this is business.

Buying Other Big-Ticket Items

Aside from houses and cars, there are other big-ticket items you may purchase such as furniture, appliances, home entertainment systems, and computer systems. Even events like weddings can be big-ticket items. Here are some tips for purchasing these items:

- Count the cost. This is particularly important if you are purchasing items on credit. An item that is reasonably priced can cost you double that if you don't have a good interest rate. Find out how much the item will cost you over the entire term—not just how much you have to pay monthly.

- Make sure the item is in alignment with your budget. Don't spend so much on big-ticket items that you can't take care of your basic living expenses: rent, utilities, clothing, and food. Only when you have an emergency reserve and the priorities discussed in chapter 3 are in place should you consider big-ticket items.

- Resist unnecessary bells and whistles. If you're not careful, you can spend a lot more than you intended on bright, shiny objects, wanting all the extras and features that you see. "Oh look, this phone will work under water and turn on the lights when I enter the house!" It's exciting to purchase the perfect house, car, computer, phone, etc. And all the features available can be particularly attractive. For this reason, be sure to set your budget before you go shopping and stick to it, regardless of how tempted you become when you arrive at the purchase location.

Once you've reached a certain level of success, you will begin to purchase more big-ticket items. The key, regardless of the type of purchase, is to do your homework, purchase within your means, and avoid getting carried away by unnecessary features that you really can't afford. Shop smart and avoid being a slave to your emotions. In the words of my late father, "Keep your yearnings within your earnings!"

17

KNOW THE RISKS AND REWARDS OF INVESTING

Money Mentoring Moment

Success in investing doesn't correlate with IQ...what you need is the temperament to control the urges that get other people into trouble in investing.

WARREN BUFFETT

Ashley, a 25-year-old single woman, just received a raise and will be taking home an extra $300 per month. She has been waiting for a chance to jump into the stock market. She heard that PPP technology is a hot stock, and she does not want to miss her opportunity to make a fast profit. She would love to be married and financially strengthened by her husband, but so far Mr. Right has not surfaced so she wants to be proactive in securing her future.

Ella, 37, has two teenaged girls, ages 14 and 16. She and her husband have managed to save over $50,000 and are looking to maximize their return on it; the funds currently sit in a savings account at their local bank earning 1.3 percent annually. Their 16-year-old will enter college in a couple of years, hopefully with at least a partial scholarship. A portion of their savings will be needed to subsidize her education.

Lenora, 58, a former pastor's wife, recently received $200,000 from her late husband's life insurance proceeds. She has no idea where to invest it or whom to trust to do so. For now she has parked the money in a 90-day certificate of deposit. Other than her modest salary from her part-time job, she will need to rely on the insurance proceeds for basic living expenses until such time that she can draw Social Security benefits. Fortunately, her living expenses are relatively low, as her home and car have been paid in full.

All of the women above desire to invest their funds, but like many, they are not sure what to invest in or how to get started. Is this your story? Well, you've come to the right chapter. Let's look at some key questions and considerations for smart investing.

What Is Your goal?

Investing is about putting money aside for a certain time so that it will grow and allow you to achieve a specific goal or purpose later. Goals are unique to each individual. Some people simply want to leave an inheritance to their dependents or chosen beneficiaries. Others want to take a dream vacation, fund educational expenses (for their children or themselves), pay down on a house, or retire with a certain amount of money in reserve so that they can enjoy a certain quality of life post-employment. Your goal will determine *how* you invest since the time horizon varies for different goals. So it's important that you get clarity on your reason for investing.

What Is Your Investment Horizon?

Lenora, the 58-year-old widow, should be concerned primarily about protecting her investment because she will need the money to live on—within a few years. She would be unwise to invest her entire $200,000 insurance proceeds in the volatile stock market. She needs to hire a financial advisor to help her develop a diversified portfolio that will align with her upcoming cash needs. Thirty-seven-year-old Ella can't really afford to take more risks because she is going to need at least half the money in the next two years for her daughter's education; however, she can get a higher return on the idle funds than what she is earning from the savings account. Finally, 25-year-old Ashley has at least 40 years to work on saving for retirement and can afford to take more risk. However, buying a single stock is not a good idea, as I will explain below (see "Mutual Funds"). *The shorter your time frame ("investment horizon") for reaching your goal, the more conservative you must be. The longer your time frame, the more risk you can take.* So ask yourself, "How much time do I have to reach my investment goal or the point at which I need access to the funds?"

How Much Can You Afford to Invest?

This is where total awareness of your core living expenses and of where you stand with respect to debts and obligations become critical. An investment is not designed to be a readily accessible piggy bank. Consider such funds as locked away and not available for daily use. Thus, you must think about how long you can survive without touching your investment. Jumping into investing before establishing an emergency fund is an unwise move. If you do, you may find yourself needing to sell the investment shortly after you make it and thereby trigger unexpected taxes. If you are still paying 13 to 26 percent interest rates on credit cards or other debt, it is wiser to pay them off before investing. However, if your employer is providing any level of matching funds for your retirement, always, always participate to the maximum; if the company matches three percent, you must invest your three percent. Matching is a 100 percent return on each dollar invested; nowhere else are you likely to ever earn such a return. Please don't be foolish by leaving this free money on the table.

What Is Your Risk Tolerance?

After you have determined your goal, how long you have to accomplish it, and how much you have available to invest, the key issue that you must settle is your tolerance for risk. All investments will carry some element of risk. You must decide how much risk you can stomach without staying up at night worrying if you will lose your money. Your risk tolerance level is a very personal decision. There are several online quizzes and questionnaires that will help you determine your risk appetite. I took the simple quiz at *https://njaes.rutgers.edu/money/riskquiz/* and learned (actually, confirmed) that I have an average/moderate tolerance for risk. Based on my quiz results, the article went on to list several types of investments that would be suitable for my personality and stage in life. Let's take a quick look at basic investment options below.

Common Investment Vehicles

Your next step in preparing to invest is to determine which financial assets align with your goals. The three main concerns in any investing strategy are: (1) protection of your funds ("safety of capital"), the growth of the investment ("capital appreciation"), and the earnings that you can expect to receive ("current income"). Financial assets fall into the following categories:

Cash and Cash Equivalents

Beyond checking and savings accounts, the following investments are key components of an investment portfolio:

Certificate of Deposit (CD): This is a promissory note issued by a bank with a fixed maturity date and a fixed interest rate. When you invest in a CD, access to the funds is restricted until the maturity date. Short-term (30 days to one year) and long-term (up to 10 years) maturities are available. The longer the CD term, the higher the interest rate. If you withdraw funds before the maturity date, there will be a penalty equal to three to six months of interest depending on the term of the CD. CDs often have a minimum deposit requirement.

The interest earned accumulates and is paid on the maturity date. For example, suppose you purchase a two-year, $10,000 CD at two percent interest compounded annually. At the end of one year, the CD will be worth $10,200; at the end of two years, the CD will be worth $10,404 (interest is computed on two percent times $10,200). This is an example of how compound interest works; interest is earned on the interest you have earned—not just the initial investment amount.

Money Market Accounts: This is a type of savings account that pays a higher interest rate than a regular savings account. Since it allows limited check writing and withdrawals, a money market account is a hybrid of a savings and checking account. Higher interest rates are offered because of the higher deposit required.

The Federal Deposit Insurance Corporation (FDIC) insures up to $250,000 per depositor, per FDIC-insured member bank, per ownership category. Deposits held in different ownership categories are separately insured, up to at least $250,000, *even if held at the same bank.* Besides checking and savings accounts, ownership categories include living trusts, revocable trust accounts, payable on death (POD) accounts, corporate accounts, and others.

Because of the FDIC guarantee, these investments are virtually risk-free—and the return (interest rate) is very low. Further, the accounts are liquid (quickly converted into cash). But they do pose a temptation to use them unnecessarily if you are not financially disciplined. Interest earned on the investments is taxable.

Bonds

Bonds are fixed-income securities that are based on debt. Purchasing a bond means you are lending your money to the issuer, which could be the federal, state, or local ("municipal") government, or a corporation. The issuer will pay interest on the bonds semiannually, providing a steady income stream, and pay back the principal amount on the bond maturity date. Bonds can have maturity terms from 1 to 30 years. The longer the term, the higher the interest rate—as with CDs and money market accounts. The interest you earn on bonds is generally taxable; interest on municipal bonds is exempt from federal income tax. Here is an example of how a bond works: X Corporation wants to build a new hospital. The company issues a $100 million, 10-year bond at 5 percent interest payable semiannually. Various investors buy a certain number of bond certificates. They collect their interest payments at 2.5 percent semiannually. At the end of 10 years when the bonds mature, X Corporation pays back the final interest payment and their initial investment. However, some investors may not wish to wait the entire 10 years, so they sell their bonds to other investors who did not participate in the original issue of the bonds.

The bonds are rated based on the issuer's creditworthiness. The top two credit rating agencies, Moody's Investors Service and Standard & Poor's (S&P), have "grading" systems that indicate the issuer's current creditworthiness. Bonds are relatively safe, with a US Treasury bond being the safest of all since it is backed by the full faith and credit of the US government—which can raise taxes to pay its bills. The return is pretty low—consistent with the low risk. (Go to *www.bankrate.com* for daily updates on current rates.) Bonds with low credit ratings pay higher rates to compensate bond buyers for taking more risk.

Interest rates and bond prices have an opposite relationship: When one goes up, the other goes down. When new bonds are issued, they typically carry an interest ("coupon") rate at or close to the prevailing market interest rate.

Bond prices are determined by market demand, the interest rate on the bond, and the bond issuer's credit rating. If a bond is trading at a discount, the market price is less than $1,000 per bond; if the market price is more than $1,000 per bond, it is being traded at a "premium."

You can purchase bonds by setting up an account with a brokerage firm such as Ally Invest, TD Ameritrade, and others. You can even buy US Treasury bonds direct (*www.treasurydirect.gov/*) and avoid the commissions and fees you would normally pay the brokerage firm.

Stocks

Purchasing stocks makes you part owner of a company. You make money by receiving a portion of the profits ("dividends") or by selling the stock when its price increases ("appreciates"). Stocks fluctuate in value on a daily basis, and stockholders are not guaranteed the return of their investment or any earnings. Further, not all stocks pay dividends. Some companies choose to reinvest the earnings back into the company for more growth.

Because of the risks involved, stocks have the potential for high return. The bottom line is that over a long term, say at least ten years, stocks have outperformed all other investments. But I must remind you that you must commit to a long investment horizon.

The stock market has two main aspects: the *primary market* and the *secondary market*. The primary market is where new shares are first sold through initial public offerings (IPOs). Institutional investors (pension funds, insurance companies, etc.) typically purchase most of these shares from the investment bank group that managed the IPO. All subsequent trading goes on in the *secondary* market, where participants include both institutional and individual investors. A company uses money raised from its IPO to grow. However, once its stock starts trading, it does not receive funds from the buying and selling of its shares between investors. The stock trading between investors occurs on "stock exchanges." The two largest in the world are the New York Stock Exchange, located on Wall Street in New York City, where traders physically buy and sell shares auction-style on the floor of the exchange, and Nasdaq, where trades only occur electronically.

The stock market's activity is a key gauge of the health of the US economy. Each weekday brings stock market report cards. Most people rely on certain indexes to interpret the results. The two most popular are the Dow Jones Industrial Average and the Standard & Poor's 500 (S&P 500). The daily Dow index represents the price of the stocks of the 30 largest, most solid "blue chip" (dividend paying) companies in the United States. The S&P 500 is comprised of the 500 leading companies from a wide range of industries. It captures 75 percent of the American stock market. Many of the companies on the list are well-known names, like Exxon, Johnson & Johnson, and Apple. The companies listed on the Dow Jones index are also part of the S&P 500.

Stock values fluctuate daily so you cannot get in a panic when you hear they are down. Remember, you are in for the long haul.

Mutual Funds

This is a collection of stocks and/or bonds that you purchase along with a group of other investors. Mutual funds often have a specific investment strategy based on specific criteria such as the size of the company, certain industries, government bonds, company bonds, and a mix of stocks and bonds. The benefit of mutual funds is that someone else will handle the selection and management of your investments and free you up to enjoy your life. These funds also give you the opportunity to invest in companies whose share price may be too high for your budget, but because you have a share in the fund, you can still participate in the stock. This would be the best move for Ashley, whom you met at the beginning of the chapter. It would be a very unwise move for her to invest in the single "hot stock" that she is so excited about.

There are three basic ways to purchase mutual funds: (1) through your self-directed retirement account, (2) directly through the financial institutions that offer them, or (3) through an online brokerage account via respected sites such as *TDAmeritrade.com* and *Etrade.com*.

The most popular mutual fund, the S&P 500, buys shares in the Standard & Poor's list of 500 or so companies that best represent the US economy. Some of the shares in these companies cost hundreds of dollars each, so it makes no sense for you to try to buy their individual stocks when you can buy into a mutual fund that buys the stock.

Your Portfolio

Your investment portfolio consists of all your assets and various investment vehicles. A portfolio can be moderate or aggressive. As previously discussed, if you have a longer investment horizon and an average risk tolerance, you may want to be moderately aggressive, seeking a balance of risk and return. A typical *conservative* portfolio may consist of 70 to 75 percent bonds/fixed-income securities, 15 to 20 percent stocks, and 5 to 15 percent cash, certificates of deposits, or other liquid assets. On the other hand, an *aggressive* portfolio may consist of 50 to 55 percent stocks, 35 to 40 percent bonds, and 5 to 10 percent cash and equivalents. Diversifying your portfolio is smart investing. If one security suffers a decline, your whole portfolio won't be at risk. It's a simple matter of not "putting all your eggs in one basket."

Your investment portfolio won't be like everyone else's, nor should it be. Take into consideration your risk tolerance level and your objectives to assemble the portfolio that will meet your needs. Every day you spend not investing is a day that you have lost an opportunity to grow your money. The smart way to invest is to save regularly, look for investments with low administrative fees, and expect to stay in the market for the long-term (at least ten years). And above all, never stop learning.

Because my goal here is to give you an overview, I highly recommend that you read Investopedia's "Investing 101: A Tutorial for Beginner Investors," a free online resource at *www.investopedia.com* for a detailed discussion of other aspects of investing in stocks, bonds, and mutual funds. Also, for a practice run to assess your current investment skills, try Investopedia's investment simulator at *www.investopedia.com/simulator*. There you can start a mock portfolio with $100,000 in virtual money in an account that actually tracks the stock market. This exercise can help you see what kind of stomach you have for investing before you invest any of your real money.

Investing maximizes your earning potential because you no longer have to trade your time for money. You can put your money to work conservatively, moderately, or aggressively. Never stop paying attention to your monthly investment statement. Know where you are invested. Monitor your portfolio to see, due to market fluctuations, if you have become too heavily invested in stocks or other risky investments or if you aren't invested enough. It's essential to understand the risks and rewards of investing so you can make informed decisions as you plan for your financial future. Stay awake here!

18

EXPLORE ENTREPRENEURSHIP

Money Mentoring Moment

Running your own business can take the limits off your earnings potential—or the blouse off your back. Before you take the plunge, know the pluses and the pitfalls of "doing your own thing."

Entrepreneurship is an American dream—or a fantasy for many, and a nightmare for others. Nothing sounds more exciting than running your own business instead of having to work at a nine-to-five job for someone else. For many women, the idea can be even more alluring, as we must often deal with difficulties in the workplace that men tend not to face, including sexual harassment, gender discrimination, and unequal pay. Further, women who desire to be home with their children but still need to make an income or want more freedom in their personal life also find the flexibility of entrepreneurship appealing.

Women's entrepreneurship has been on the rise in the United States since 1997. Women-owned businesses now account for 39 percent of all US firms. As of January 2017, there are an estimated 11.6 million women-owned businesses that employ nearly 9 million people and generate more than $1.7 trillion in revenues.[1] Our time has arrived.

The Pluses of Entrepreneurship

If you are stuck in a dead-end job, bored with your daily routine, or have a hobby or idea that could produce income, perhaps you may want to consider the following benefits of entrepreneurship:

- *Control:* One of the most compelling benefits of being an entrepreneur is the control you have over your work priorities and style.

- *Flexibility:* When you work for yourself, your schedule is your own. Some days I work 4 hours; other times it's more like 14. The good news is that I can take off at will to rest up for the excessive hours. I schedule my medical and other personal appointments to my convenience. And many days I work in my pajamas. Flexibility is a huge benefit.

- *Financial freedom:* Although it may take time to build up to a significant level of revenue, most entrepreneurs ultimately make more money than they did in their regular jobs.

- *Personal fulfillment:* When you start your own business, you are free to indulge in your passions and fulfill lifelong dreams rather than working for an employer whose values you may not embrace.

- *Time management:* As a work-at-home author, my commute is approximately 30 feet from my bedroom. Obviously, my productivity is a lot better than it would be if I worked in a cubicle where I'd be interrupted every few minutes. Or if I were sitting in traffic on a busy freeway.

- *Increased confidence:* Starting an endeavor and seeing it through instills confidence. Running a business often involves dealing with challenges and making the hard decisions, but mastering the difficult tasks can spur you on to do even bigger things. Success produces confidence.

The Realities of "Doing Your Own Thing"

As a full-time entrepreneur for more than a decade at the time of this writing, I have had a rewarding experience. Lest I have painted too rosy a picture here for "doing your own thing," let me balance our discussion with a dose of reality. While the concept of entrepreneurship sounds like utopia, you would be wise to consider what I call the "M-Factors" before taking the plunge:

The Mentality

Determine whether you have an entrepreneurial mind-set by answering the following questions:

- Are you at least a moderate risk taker? Entrepreneurs take risks!

- Are you an initiator, or do you perform better if someone winds you up and puts you on the track? This is not a knock against your character or intelligence. Some people are just better followers than leaders.

- Can you motivate, manage, and evaluate employees—and terminate those whose goals and behavior do not align with your vision?

- Are you decisive, or do you tend to mull over a decision long after you have considered the facts and gotten advice from others?

- Are you intimidated by employees who are more capable than you?

- Do you harbor prejudices or stereotypes about the abilities or tendencies of certain sexes, races, or ethnic groups?

- Are you comfortable asking for favor or to be exempt from "normal policies" when you need special consideration in a transaction?

- Are you flexible and receptive to change, or do you tend to cling to a plan of action once you have developed it?

- Are you a problem solver who faces a challenge without whining or stressing?

- Can you admit your mistakes to others without feeling diminished?

- Do you confront a conflict in a timely manner, or do you delay with the hope it will go away?

- Are you willing to solicit and listen to the input of others?

- Do you have a stick-to-it attitude and persist in the face of adversity?

- Are you willing to network faithfully to advance your business?

If you answered "no" to any of these questions, you might want to consider whether becoming an entrepreneur is right for you. Nevertheless, even if you determine that you may not be ready now, that doesn't mean you'll never be. This exercise may have simply helped you identify a few weak areas you need to strengthen.

The Market

Every business idea is not marketable. Does your product or service meet a need in the marketplace? Is your idea an innovative, proprietary approach to solving a problem in a way that no one else has addressed? Are you improving upon an existing product or service? There are several ways to determine if you have a good idea:

- Research current industry trends. It is critical to know the trends that will affect your market so that you can be sure that your proposed product or service will be viable in the future. Every business must adapt to the changing desires and behaviors of consumers. There are tons of Internet sites that can guide you in your search. Simply go to *Google.com* and type in "trends in the (your) industry."

- Evaluate the competition. Know which businesses are dominating the market currently and how your product or service will improve upon their efforts. It is true that occasionally someone comes up with an idea that no one else has implemented, but for the most part, someone else is already in business doing what you want to do. So you must be clear on how to make your product or service unique. If you are not the research type, you may just have to hire a marketing professional to assist you. Therefore, build your financial resources so that you can afford to hire the expertise you need. Be sure to get good referrals on the person or firm's track record before you hire them.

The Management

When I worked as a VP at a venture capital firm, we held fast to our theory that the quality of the management team was the most critical factor in deciding whether to invest in a company. We believed the greatest idea in the world will fail if you don't have the right people to execute the main aspects of the operation: planning, production, administration, marketing, and accounting/finance. As you ponder your business idea, get clarity from others as to how much help you will need. Many entrepreneurs start out as the sole employee; however, you will eventually need the help of others because you simply can't do everything. This doesn't necessarily mean hiring employees. Initially, your team may consist of a few key independent contractors, such as virtual assistants, graphic artists, a web designer, etc., which you can hire at reasonable, "satisfaction guaranteed or your credit card not charged" rates on sites like *Upwork.com*, *Freelancer .com*, and others.

The Money

There is not a single enterprise that does not require some level of start-up costs. You will surely need funds for equipment, supplies, advertising, and other essential expenses. Depending on what industry you choose, these expenditures can be substantial. Where do you look for capital? Your personal savings? Family? Friends? Yup! There is still much gender bias in the area of funding women's businesses. Thus, a huge majority of women will have to bring their own funds to the table. Your chance of getting a loan from a bank is pretty slim unless you plan to obtain a home equity loan (while still employed). Banks generally do not finance start-ups because of the high risk of failure. I highly recommend against encumbering your home. It will probably be your most significant asset toward your retirement, so think twice before exposing it to risk.

Consider pursuing the business part-time if you can do so and remain effective in your regular job. This option lowers your risks, as you will have time to test the waters before you take the plunge into full-time entrepreneurship. Once your sideline becomes profitable and starts to interfere with your job, it just may be time to give notice. I took this path personally when I left my job as a chief financial officer of an organization to become a full-time writer and speaker.

To get positioned financially, my husband and I eliminated all credit card debt, got a firm grip on our core household expenses, projected a conservative amount to be earned from speaking and book sales, and left space in the planning for God's favor and intervention. As a woman of faith, you can indeed take a "faith step" if you feel God is leading you to. You do not have to have *all* the bases covered before you obey Him. It sounds trite, but it's true: "Where He guides, He provides." It is also important to walk in integrity toward your employer and not to cheat the company of any time you are paid for. That means you should not work on your business on company time; do not sow seeds of dishonesty, for you will surely reap what you sow. I believe God honored my commitment to my employer in this manner by surrounding me with unprecedented favor with clients, media, consumers, and others after I made my departure.

Funding your dream may indeed be a major hurdle, but don't despair. Leave no stone unturned. Always keep good relations with family and friends, and keep your word, especially when it comes to financial matters. Should you seek a loan from one of them, make every effort to honor the terms of your written agreement. If a later due date or other adjustment is needed, be prompt in advising them. Don't go silent when people have trusted you with their money.

The Mode

Before you open for business, you will need to understand the various modes of business operations or structures available so you can choose the right one for the nature and stage of your enterprise. The structure you choose has a direct impact on your personal liability, income taxes, and administrative costs of complying with the structure. Here is an overview of the most common modes of operation:

Sole Proprietorship. This is the simplest and easiest to form type of business structure. You may operate under your name or a "DBA" (doing business as) cleared by your local government. The entity is controlled by one person—you. The business income is taxed at the individual level. As a sole proprietor, you are personally responsible for the company's liabilities. Thus, your personal assets will be at risk.

Regular Corporation (also known as a C corporation). A corporation is an independent entity, separate from its owners. A corporation is more complex and expensive to form and is subject to more regulations and tax requirements. You incorporate your enterprise by filing Articles of Incorporation with the appropriate agency in your state. Upon incorporation, you must issue yourself common stock in exchange for whatever assets (cash, equipment, vehicles, etc.) you are transferring to the corporation. You must also elect a board of directors and comply with the state's requirement to hold annual meetings. Most people just starting out won't begin under this structure unless their product or service is susceptible to lawsuits (e.g., food-related enterprises or products that are the result of creative thought like recordings, copyright materials, patents, etc.). For example, if you are in the business of making custom quilts, your risk of being sued is a lot lower than Sally's Gourmet Soups.

The key advantages of the corporate mode of operation include the following:

- The owner's personal assets are protected from damages assessed to the corporation.
- The corporation can raise capital by selling its stock to others. You will definitely need to be incorporated if you plan to approach venture capitalist or private investors.

Caution: Often, cash-strapped entrepreneurs offer stock in exchange for services during the initial start-up of the company. Remember that stock is ownership; don't give up equity so quickly. I once had two ladies, unable to find capital from other sources, offer me 30 percent of their business in exchange for putting together a proposal for private financing for them. I refused to take advantage of their naiveté. Only offer stock as a last resort—when you have exhausted all other options.

- More benefits can be offered to the owners and more categories of expenses can be deducted.

A significant *disadvantage* of a corporation is that the owners/stockholders are subject to double taxation on income earned from the same source. You see, the corporation pays taxes on its net earnings. Then when it distributes those earnings to stockholders in the form of dividends, the stockholders must pay taxes on the dividends received. Small corporations where the owners work as employees often declare themselves bonuses to wipe out the net income and eliminate the taxes. Don't try this strategy without guidance from a tax professional.

It is critical that you invest the time and money to get professional advice on when (or if) to incorporate, as many entrepreneurs jump the gun in doing so and incur unnecessary fees and state assessments.

S Corporation. Entrepreneurs electing this structure enjoy the same protected status as that of a C corporation. However, the income and losses are passed through to the shareholders and taxed at their personal tax rates. If the stockholders work for the company, they must pay themselves a reasonable salary (and deduct the required Social Security taxes) before they can declare themselves a dividend. This is a smart strategy for some people since dividends are not subject to Social Security taxes, withholding, or company matching.

Limited Liability Company (LLC). This type of structure is a hybrid entity that combines the best features of a partnership (explained below) and a corporation. It protects the owners' assets without the double taxation of corporations. Earnings and losses pass through to the owners and are included on their personal tax returns. This structure is similar to an S corporation, but it provides more benefits to the owners. If you set up a limited liability company, you may be required to file articles of organization, which act as a charter to establish the existence of your LLC in your state and set forth certain basic information about the new business. You may be required to file an Operating Agreement with the state as well, which outlines the ownership and member duties of your limited liability company and allows you to set out the financial and working relations among business owners.

Partnership. A partnership is formed when two or more people get together to jointly create a business. There are basically two types of partnerships: general and limited. In a general partnership, all the partners share in the liability and management of the entity. In a limited partnership, there must be at least one general partner. The limited partners are usually providing only capital and do not participate in the daily operations. Their personal liability for the entity's debts is limited to how much they have invested. For example, if you are a limited partner who has invested $50,000 and the partnership is held liable for damages in a $500,000 lawsuit, the most that you could ever be responsible for is $50,000.

For tax purposes, the partnership passes its profits and losses to the individual partners. Like sole proprietors, general partners are responsible for the liabilities or damages assessed the business.

Caution! If you are considering going into a partnership with a friend or family member, be careful to consider more than just the business skills and finances of your potential partner. Take time to evaluate whether you are "unequally yoked"—emotionally, morally, or spiritually. The phrase "unequally yoked" goes back to an Old Testament law in Deuteronomy 22:10 that prohibits plowing with an ox and a donkey yoked together. The idea is that you've got two different animals with different mind-sets and goals. Therefore, they will be ineffective in their mutual assignment. In the same way, your business can only be effective when you partner with someone of like mind. Don't put your head in the sand on troubling character flaws you have observed. Consider whether your partner shares the same beliefs, values, and goals. Paul warns us in 2 Corinthians 6:14-15 (NLT) about such alliances:

> Don't team up with those who are unbelievers. How can righteousness be a partner with wickedness? How can light live with darkness? What harmony can there be between Christ and the devil? How can a believer be a partner with an unbeliever?

Starting your own business is risky. It takes time, commitment, know-how, and money. Some women do not count the costs before they take the plunge. Many women have the qualifications but lack the confidence to "step out of the boat." Once you are fully persuaded that you want to go this route, be sure that you have adequately prepared yourself with enough basic information to at least ask relevant questions. It will be money well spent to pay for an hour or two with a reputable business consultant to discuss the pluses and pitfalls for your particular enterprise. It would be equally wise to enroll in an entrepreneur course and learn the basics of running a business.

Part 5

PREPARE FOR PROBLEMS AND PITFALLS

19

RECOGNIZE SCAMMERS AND TAKERS

Money Mentoring Moment

We all want that one big break that will provide a substantial financial windfall and set us up for life, but we must become aware of the telltale signs that shout, "Too good to be true!"

When we hear about various financial scams, we often think it can only happen to those who aren't savvy enough to know better than to fall for dishonest tactics of others. But anyone can fall victim to financial fraud. Aside from scams involving technology or identity theft, it is often greed or desperation that sets one up to be a victim.

Emotions can cause us to make impulsive spending decisions or fall for get-rich-quick schemes. Scammers rely on the emotional decisions of others to be successful in their endeavors. They count on the victim making a quick decision, which is why they often emphasize acting "right now." Greed and desperation cause people to make an irrational decision because they don't want to miss out on a good thing.

In Luke 12:15, Jesus gives this warning: "Watch out! Be on your guard against all kinds of greed; life does not consist in an abundance of possessions."

Popular Scams

Do your homework and become aware of the various scams being perpetrated today. This can go a long way toward arming you for defense against them.

Identity Theft

In a world that has been taken over by technology, it's more important than ever to protect your identity. Technology can be a blessing and a curse. It has made it so easy for criminals to steal your identity by using your address, credit card or bank account information, or Social Security number. They can use your identity to obtain credit or loans in your name, access funds in your personal bank account and credit cards, and even steal your income tax refund. The best way to protect yourself is to do the following:

- Keep your important documents in a safe place.
- Shred paperwork you no longer need that contains sensitive information.
- Check your mail as soon as possible; don't leave your mail unattended for long periods of time.
- Use secure passwords while doing business online.
- Periodically review your accounts or sign up for an alert service to notify you of suspicious activity.
- Monitor your credit report to make sure it contains nothing you don't recognize. *AnnualCreditReport.com* allows you to check your report from all three bureaus once a year for free.

IRS/Government Scams

Everyone's afraid of the Internal Revenue Service, so scammers often take advantage of that. Someone will call and inform you that you owe the government money, encouraging you to wire the funds to them or send a prepaid debit card. These unorthodox payment requests should alert you that something is not right. Government agencies don't operate this way. Before agreeing to send any money, hang up and directly call the government agency to verify the debt.

E-mail Scams

There is a common scam in which the perpetrators spin an elaborate story about a large sum of money that is tied up due to problems in a certain country—or even a personal hardship or dilemma. They need to quickly transfer the money out, and they need your help to do it. But in exchange, they will allow you to keep a hefty portion. They ask for your bank information to transfer the funds, but of course, those funds never arrive. You can avoid these scams by not falling for sob stories from people you don't know.

Senior Scams

Seniors are often victims of financial scams, as they are perceived as easy marks. Some senior scams include the following:

- *Medicare scams:* A person will call the senior pretending to be from the Medicare office. They ask for personal information, claiming they need it to update the account. In reality, they are seeking information to steal the senior's identity.

- *Investment scams:* Because seniors are often planning for or are concerned about their retirement, they are easy prey for investment scams. The scammers promise to invest the senior's money while promising an over-the-top lucrative return; however, they steal the money rather than invest it, often taking everything the senior has.

- *Lottery scams:* The scammer alerts the senior that they have won a large sum of money. The only catch is that they have to pay a significant fee to access this money.

Since seniors are particularly vulnerable to such scams, the best prevention is education and having people in the family to turn to regarding important decisions.

Family Hardship Scams

Some scammers prey on the emotions of their targets to obtain money. They call someone and pretend they are calling on behalf of a family member in immediate need of cash. If anyone calls you for cash about a relative, be sure you know whom you are talking to, and never send money to a third party. Make a phone call yourself to determine whether there is a valid need.

Employment Scams

People who work from home are often targets of those who perpetrate employment scams. These ads often promise a salary of thousands a week for very little effort, and they sound more like sales ads than employment ads. Other types of ads read like employment ads, even using the correct terminology for the industry. However, during the interview, which is often by phone or Skype, they reveal that you need to first purchase the equipment necessary to do the job. The interviewer assures you they will pay for it. All you have to do is deposit a large check into your bank account and use some of the money to purchase the equipment (often from the same person you are talking to). The check bounces, but you have already sent the money to the scammer. You should never be asked to pay your employer, regardless of what they say the money is for. And never cash large checks from people or companies you don't know, especially if you are asked to send some of it back.

Dating Scams

The computer and the rise of the Internet have contributed to the rise of online dating. The problem is that people often conduct the entire romance online, in many cases not meeting the other party in person. Unfortunately, people can hide behind the computer screen and pretend to be someone they are not. These scammers prey on lonely people, make them fall in love, and then hit them up for money in various ways. The solution is to be cautious or resolve to date the old-fashioned way, in person, and avoid falling victim to the insincere flattery of online suitors.

Computer Repair Scams

Your computer is apparently "compromised" in some way, but you don't know it until some helpful person contacts you about the problem. In this popular scam, they may ask to take over your computer or have you pay them a fee via your credit card or bank account. These scammers may contact you by phone, but they are more likely to use a popup on your computer that requests that you call the number on the screen for a resolution. Avoid falling for this, as remote companies don't have a way of determining that you have a virus or any other computer problem before you give them access.

Debt Collection Scams

Debt collection scams bank on the desire of people to pay their bills. They tell you that you owe a fake debt and convince you that you must pay now. When you agree to make a payment, you are then asked to pay via a wire transfer or another untraceable method. You can avoid this by knowing exactly what debts you owe. If you don't recognize the company, or you recognize the company but not the amount of your supposed debt, do some research first.

Credit Repair Scams

Many companies exist that offer to provide you a brand-new credit profile, which will effectively give you a brand-new slate on which to build credit and allow you to leave your old credit issues behind. To facilitate this, the company suggests that you obtain an Employee Identification Number to use in place of your Social Security number. But this is illegal and you would be wise not to use the services of such companies. Recognize that there's no easy or quick way to fix your credit, and be determined to make the effort to do it the right way.

Beware of Red Flags

All scams, regardless of the type, have many things in common. If you know what to look for, you will be ahead of the game when people try to run their game on you. Look out for these red flags to avoid falling victim to the unscrupulous tactics of scammers:

- Your instincts tell you to run. You know the old saying, "If it looks like a duck, swims like a duck, and quacks like a duck, it's probably a duck." Don't be naïve, and don't ignore your instincts. Ask questions until you feel comfortable; if you don't feel comfortable, avoid moving forward.

- You are being pressured to "act now." Legitimate businesses may urge you to act now as well, so this can be a tricky one. But scammers kick the urgency into full gear. The deal will sound so good that you are afraid of losing it and thus give in to the pressure. If you're ever feeling particularly pressured, ask for 24 hours to think about it and note the response you receive. Often you will hear an excuse for why it can't wait that long.

- You are asked to provide personal information. Many businesses do have a legitimate need for some personal information when you call them. But if you receive an unsolicited call from a business you have had no previous contact with, you shouldn't provide any information. This is the scammer's way of fishing for details they can use to steal your identity.

- You can't obtain any contact information. If you happen to make contact with someone you suspect is involved in fraud, try making plans to call them back in a few hours. If they won't provide their company name, department, and phone number, it's a sign that you shouldn't conduct any business with them.

- You are approved for a loan but must pay a fee. If someone contacts you offering guaranteed approval for a loan or credit card, you shouldn't have to pay a fee upfront. They should be giving you money!

Saying No to Takers

Takers aren't necessarily scammers. They are people you know, such as friends and family, who take advantage of your good nature and always have their hand out. Perhaps you have a friend who always wants to borrow money or an adult child who always expects you to help pay a bill every month. Maybe you have a friend who regularly sticks you with the bill when you go out to eat. Once you see a pattern of those who consistently try to take advantage of you, don't delay in putting safeguards in place to protect your finances.

Begin setting firm boundaries. Implement a "no loan" policy. Only pay your share at dinner. Simply review the bill, put your share on the table, and continue socializing. Say no to your adult child, and stop enabling them to remain financially immature. This doesn't mean that you can't help people who are genuinely in need; God expects us to have giving hearts.

Being a Christian doesn't mean we should allow people to walk all over us, nor does it mean we shouldn't ask the hard questions when considering a financial transaction. We are to be good stewards over that which God has entrusted to us, and part of being a good steward is preventing folks from separating you from your money. Proverbs 2:12 advises, "Wisdom will save you from the ways of wicked men, from men whose words are perverse."

Molly's Story

I owned a car that was beginning to require more and more repairs. My mechanic suggested I stop putting more money into it as it was old and would continue to be a financial drain. I decided to sell it, so I made the critical repairs and also bought new tires. John, the man I was dating, asked me if I would sell it to his friend Roland. I was honest with John and shared the mechanic's assessment. Although I was reluctant, John persuaded me to sell to Roland. He promised to collect the payments from him on my behalf. Although I didn't know Roland, I trusted John. I gave Roland the car and the pink slip without getting payment.

Throughout the following six months that John and I dated, I never received a penny. Whenever I would ask about the money, John would respond, "Oh, he's been having problems with the car. Let me talk to him."

After we broke up, I emailed John for an update on the transaction. I also told him I had received the registration notice. Apparently I had failed to complete the transfer of the title to Roland's name. This created a huge liability for me. I either needed to get payment for the car or get it back. John politely informed me that he was removing himself from the situation and that any future follow-up was now between Roland and me. So six months after releasing the car along with the pink slip, I confronted Roland about the uncollected debt. He was shocked and told me he thought John had paid me the money. Roland informed me he had no funds to repay me and that the car was not in working condition.

I learned later after speaking to my mechanic that Roland had brought the car to him for repairs. It needed a new engine because he had been driving it with no coolant. Thus, the car was not working due to his negligence. I made arrangements to have it towed to a junkyard, at a cost of $300. Had I sold it to anyone else, I would have gotten at least $1,900. I was very disappointed that these two men (whom others esteem as reputable because of their leadership positions at church) had blatantly refused to honor their word. I felt totally taken advantage of. Ultimately, I left it in God's hands. One day we will all reap what we sow.

I was fuming by the time Molly finished telling me her story. I asked her what lessons she had learned from this whole ordeal. Before she responded to the question, she said, "Oh, I'm involved in another situation similar to this one." She proceeded to relate another incident with a similar outcome. It is safe to say, we have found the enemy of Molly's finances—and it is she!

20

DEAL WITH THE UNEXPECTED

Money Mentoring Moment

Although we are to walk by faith, life happens. We are not exempt from the reality of unexpected events; however, wise women "see danger and take refuge, but the simple keep going and pay the penalty" (Proverbs 22:3).

The righteous person shall live by faith, so says Galatians 3:11. Many people erroneously interpret this to mean they don't need to plan for the future. They live by faith and are trusting God to meet their need when it arises. But the Bible also says that we should foresee the evil and take refuge (Proverbs 22:3). This means planning for potentially negative situations before they occur and taking steps to minimize your loss.

There are a number of ways to prepare for the unexpected, including getting insurance, preparing a will or living trust, and planning for disability.

Essential Insurance Policies

Insurance policies don't prevent the occurrence of a loss, but they do protect us from financial loss if we happen to incur one. Following are the five necessary types of insurance:[1]

Health Insurance

Medical expenses can be huge between routine doctors' visits, emergency room visits, and daily medication. For this reason, health insurance is a must. In 2009, over 60 percent of all personal bankruptcies were related to health insurance costs. If you don't already have health insurance, it's wise to fix that problem now. Waiting until you are sick will result in higher premiums, or even worse, prevent you from being insured at all.

Car Insurance

Almost every state requires that you have car insurance. This protects other drivers and the damage to their vehicle in case you cause an accident. Insurance also protects you and your vehicle, allowing you to obtain necessary medical treatment, get your vehicle repaired, or even replace your car if it is totaled or stolen.

Homeowner's/Renter's Insurance

Homeowner's insurance protects your home against damage and theft, though you may need extra coverage against fire, flooding, and other disasters. Renter's insurance protects the personal items in your home. If you lose your valuable items in a fire, for instance, you would be able to replace them.

Life Insurance

Life insurance protects your family from the loss of your income when you die. It can pay for funeral and burial costs and provide for your family after you are gone. There are two main types of life insurance, whole life and term. Term life insurance provides a death benefit for a fixed term, usually ranging from 5 to 30 years. When the term is up, your coverage ends. There is no remaining value in the policy.

Whole life insurance provides a death benefit as long as you continue to pay the premium. These policies also accumulate cash value, which you can borrow against for any reason. Whole life insurance is expensive and complex; for that reason, it's not the best choice for most people.

Term life insurance is a good buy because it costs less than whole life insurance for significantly more coverage. The premium is less expensive because term life insurance has an expiration date, based on the number of years chosen for the term. Depending on your age, premiums can range from $430 to $7,300 per year.[2] If you die during the policy term, your beneficiaries will receive the full payout benefit; however, you won't receive a payout if you die after the term has ended. For this reason, it's important to switch to whole life insurance at the appropriate time. This strategy assumes you will be healthy enough to qualify for such a policy—which is the downside of buying term insurance. However, many term life insurance policies have a clause that allows conversion to whole life without evidence of insurability. That means you won't have to re-qualify for the insurance or take a physical exam. Let's say, for example, that you purchase a 20-year term life insurance with a 10-year conversion clause. In year eight, you discover you have heart disease. Because of the conversion clause, you can switch to whole life without the risk of a higher premium due to your health. Without a conversion clause, you would have to seek new insurance, which would be expensive in the event you could find a company willing to insure you. Thus, it might be wise to consider investing in a small whole life policy with at least enough coverage for the cost of a funeral—unless you plan to self-insure (pay for funeral costs from your savings).

So be sure you have a *convertible* term insurance policy, and make sure you convert it in the time allotted. Review your policy on an annual basis so the end of your term doesn't catch you off guard.

Life insurance is a smart but significant investment to make, and it is always best to take the first step from a place of knowledge. Be sure to thoroughly research the plans, rates, riders, and customer support reviews that are found online before making any decisions. *SelectQuote.com* is a great online service that compares the rates companies charge for various types of insurance.

Disability Insurance

Disability insurance offers protection in the event you are partially or totally disabled. If you are unable to work, disability insurance reimburses all or a portion of your lost income. Of all the ways to plan for the future, planning for a disability is probably the most neglected—and the most likely to occur. If you become sick, injured, or have to be out of work for a while, disability insurance provides a monetary payout so you can continue providing for your basic needs.

There are two types of disability insurance: short-term and long-term. Short-term disability insurance is typically used if you have to be out of work for several weeks, such as occurs with maternity leave. You are then paid 50 to 70 percent of your salary for the duration of your leave. Short-term disability insurance is often included as part of a company's benefit package. Long-term disability kicks in when short-term disability ends. It pays benefits for a longer term but still has limits, depending on the duration purchased. Not all employers offer long-term disability, but if they do, you would be wise to take advantage of it. It will be less expensive than obtaining it on your own.

Another thing to be on the lookout for is whether the policy is "own-occupation" or "any-occupation." An own-occupation policy means that if you can no longer perform in your current occupation, your benefits would be paid, even if you can work in another field. An "any-occupation" policy means that if you can no longer work in your current occupation but can work in a different occupation, you receive no benefits. Obviously the first is more desirable, so read the fine print to make sure you have the coverage you want. Be sure to thoroughly research the plans, rates, riders, and customer support reviews that are found online before making any decisions.

Non-Essential Insurance

Flight Insurance coverage is unnecessary. Such accidents are rare and your current life insurance policy should already provide coverage.

Life Insurance for Children is designed to protect your dependents. Children do not have "dependents." Save the money and put it in an educational fund.

Mortgage Life Insurance pays off your house in the event of your death. Rather than add another policy and another bill to your list of insurance plans, it makes more sense to get a term life policy instead that includes enough coverage to pay off the house and other bills.

Specific Disease Insurance. Even though I've known of a couple of people who benefited from policies that covered cancer, it's wiser if you are watching your budget to just get a good medical coverage policy that covers your health in general regardless of the problem you face.

Accidental-Death Insurance policies are difficult and misleading, especially to older people. Accidents and other catastrophic events are covered under other life insurance policies, so save your money and avoid this one.

Death: A Will, Trust, or Both?

There are tons of books written on this subject, but let's just get a basic understanding for now of the key differences between a will and a living trust. A will is inexpensive and easy to set up. It can actually be handwritten, witnessed, and notarized. However, the provisions of a will can be carried out only by a court order, which can be a lengthy and expensive process called "probate" lasting from 9 to 24 months or longer, depending on whether someone contests the will or not. It is a public document, so all the world can view it. The fees for the attorney and the executor are set by statute in most states depending on the size of the estate. Such fees could run as high as seven to ten percent of the value of the estate; thus, in some states a $300,000 estate may cost the heirs $30,000 to settle. Wills are the best tools for indicating the owner's desire to distribute non-titled assets such as jewelry, paintings, and special gifts, as well as for indicating their desires for funeral arrangements.

A revocable living trust is more expensive to set up but saves money in the end, and it is less costly than the statutory fees involved in a will. It gives the trustee the legal authority to distribute assets immediately to the beneficiaries based on the terms of the trust. No court proceedings are involved. No public notice of death is required as it is with a will. All that is required is a death certificate and a trust document that describes how things are to be distributed through the trust. Because there is no probate, there are no fees, and there is no public record of the value of your estate, which protects your privacy. Usually the assets are transferred to the beneficiary within 3 to 4 months versus the 9 to 24 months that it might require to probate a will. A trust is the best instrument for transferring "titled" assets (real estate, businesses, and other).

A living trust is not a necessity for everyone. It all depends on what you own, how old you are, and so forth. I simply wanted to raise your consciouness of it here and give you a quick overview of its benefits. Please seek counsel from your financial advisor as to your best course of action based on your circumstances.

A living trust may cost anywhere from $1,000 to $3,000 on average to set up. However, there are online templates unique to each state that you can use to set up your own. A smart move is to draft it and have an estate attorney review it. The primary goal of the trust is usually to avoid probate costs. But there are other ways to avoid such costs depending on the nature of the assets.

Another difference between a living trust and a will is that a living trust can be in effect while you are alive, whereas a will goes into effect only after you die.

If you choose not to hire a lawyer and want to fill out and file the forms yourself, you can get them from sites such as *LegalZoom .com*, *USLegalForms.com*, and *FindLaw.com*. But don't be pennywise and pound foolish here. Estate laws can be tricky and complicated, so consider allowing a qualified attorney to prepare these documents for you—especially if your assets consist of more than just a bank account.

So how do you know whether you need a will or a living trust? Here are some facts to consider:

With a will—

- You can name a guardian for your children.

- Your estate must go through probate, which can be expensive.

- You can't make provisions for what you desire to be done if you become incapacitated.

- Your assets will be a matter of public record.
- The court will intervene if your estate is mismanaged.

With a trust—

- You can't name a guardian for your children.
- Your estate will not have to go through probate.
- You can make provisions for your wishes in case you are incapacitated.
- You can keep your assets out of the public record.
- You can provide for young or disabled children.
- It is less likely to be contested.
- You must be able to trust the trustee, as there will be no court intervention.
- You must list each asset that you wish to have included.

No one relishes the idea of dying; therefore, most people avoid creating a will or living trust. Just know that if you die "intestate" (without a will), your assets will be distributed to your heirs according to your state's laws of "intestate succession," without regard for your wishes or the needs of your heirs. Your meanest sibling or the dad who abandoned you could end up with assets you wished to leave your caring niece or neighbor.

Deciding whether a will or a living trust is right for you depends on the size of your estate, the type of assets included, and the plans you have for your family.

Ways to Avoid Probate

Just for the record, many valuable assets do *not* have to be probated by the courts. They will pass to the surviving co-owner or to the beneficiary you have named, whether you have a will or not. Such assets include:

- Life insurance proceeds.
- Payable-on-death (POD) bank accounts (simply designate

a beneficiary on an existing bank account). I'm really big on this one because often when someone dies, the heirs need immediate cash for critical expenses and may not have access to bank accounts until the will is probated.

- Real estate held as "Joint Tenants" (versus "Tenants in Common"). See the definitions in chapter 14.

- Funds in an IRA, 401(k), 403(b), or other retirement accounts that have named beneficiaries.

- Property you have transferred to a living trust.

Recovering After a Divorce

Although God hates divorce, He is merciful and will forgive you for marrying the wrong person or for your role in why your marriage ended. No need to beat yourself up here. Be objective about what really went awry, note the lessons learned, and ask God for the grace to adopt a "next" mentality. Yes, this is simple but not easy. Therefore, don't add to your relational woes by being financially stressed as a result of a divorce. Follow these strategies for recovering after a divorce:[3]

- Avoid making major decisions—emotionally or financially. You may be tempted to find another husband right away to help shoulder the financial load, especially if you have dependent children. Moving to get away from your problems or taking a vacation could pose an additional threat to your financial stability. You may even be tempted to treat yourself to a "comfort" or luxury purchase. Don't do it. You are more responsible than that.

- Focus on the essentials. As a divorced woman, you are losing your husband's income, and possibly his financial leadership if he paid all the bills. To avoid becoming overwhelmed, focus your resources initially only on what you need to survive: shelter, food, transportation, and clothing. Let these core priorities drive your spending. Everything else can wait until you are more stable.

- Get help. After a divorce, you may find it difficult to think straight or make sense of your new financial situation. Don't be afraid to ask for help. Ask a trusted, financially responsible relative or friend to assist you. Debt counselors may be available at your church, or they can refer you to someone for assistance.

Being Prepared

Divorce isn't the only life circumstance that can leave you vulnerable. Your husband may pass away unexpectedly or become debilitated through an accident or an illness—in which case all of the previous cautions apply. Be proactive in your marriage to avoid being helpless if you suddenly find yourself on your own. Avoid allowing your husband to handle household finances without your participation. Even if he insists otherwise, stay in the loop on exactly where you stand by reviewing bank accounts and knowing the related access codes, passwords, insurance policies, etc. Be aware of all debts owed. If you are not savvy enough to handle your financial affairs, enlist the help of a trusted and financially astute friend or relative.

Although we live by faith, life happens. Disability, death, divorce, and other life disadvantages are real, and we must be prepared to address them in a financially savvy manner. You owe it to yourself and to those you love to evaluate your situation and leave your affairs in order to the best of your ability. In the event of your untimely death, your family will have enough to worry about just dealing with their emotions. You do them a disservice if they have to worry about your financial matters as well.

21

MANAGE YOUR SUCCESS

Money Mentoring Moment

*If you fail to manage the demands and expectations
of your success, you can soon become a spiritual,
relational, physical, and emotional failure.*

The more successful you become, the more important it will be to manage and monitor your priorities. Many things will try to pull you in a thousand different directions and it can be difficult to prioritize them all. My heart's desire is to follow the example of Jesus. After a long day of healings and meeting people's needs, Jesus took some time to steal away to commune with His heavenly Father. However, His disciples interrupted Him and urged Him to get back to business as usual.

> Simon and his companions went to look for him, 37 and when they found him, they exclaimed: "Everyone is looking for you!"
>
> Jesus replied, "Let us go somewhere else—to the nearby villages—so I can preach there also. That is why I have come" (Mark 1:36-38).

Like Jesus, we've got to be a broken record in keeping the main thing the main thing. Jesus could have given in to the demands of others, but He knew His priorities and was determined to fulfill them, despite the desire of the crowd.

Learning to Say No

No one wants to be a party pooper, but sometimes you must learn to say no in order to protect your spiritual, physical, emotional, and relational well-being. If you're not used to saying no, doing so may feel rude, selfish, or uncaring the first few times you try it. But practice makes perfect. It is essential to guard your time in order to maintain your success. If you don't, you will soon be focusing on everything except the main thing.

Women are particularly vulnerable to the tendency to constantly say yes. We were raised to be sweet, soft-hearted, and kind. These are not bad traits; they are actually good, but they may have been emphasized to us without the instruction that it's also okay to say no. And this is when we can fall into the trap of "yes." We think we will no longer be liked or embraced if we say no, but this is far from the truth. Those who are worth our time can handle our "no."

Here are some tips for mastering the art of saying no:[1]

- Keep your response simple. Use a firm and direct approach. Do you find yourself being overly apologetic during those times you build up the nerve to say no? If so, you can use the following phrases as practice: "Thanks for asking, but I'm afraid I can't accommodate your request."

- Buy some time. This is particularly helpful if you're prone to saying yes when put on the spot. Avoid giving an answer right away. Simply say, "Let me get back to you on that."

- It's okay to compromise. If it's something you really wouldn't mind doing, perhaps you can compromise and offer an alternative. For example, you are asked to attend a banquet for a worthy cause but you are unable to attend. You can offer to give a donation instead. However, don't offer a compromise if you really want to say no.

- Set boundaries with your children. You love your children, and it can be particularly hard to say no to them. However, they must learn that they can't always have their way. Teaching them this lesson now will help them as they transition into adulthood. And if your children are grown, the same applies. They must learn not to take advantage of your relationship; they must learn to respect your boundaries.

- Be honest with yourself. If you find yourself always saying yes and later regretting it, you aren't being true to yourself. It's okay to take the time to evaluate requests to determine how you really feel. Don't consider what the other person will think or feel. Ask yourself, "Do I want to do this or not?" Or, better yet, "Does God want me to do this?" Only by answering these questions truthfully for yourself can you respond truthfully to others.

Say Good-bye to Busyness

If you're always busy, that's a good thing, right? It means you're getting things done. Actually, you don't have to be chronically busy to accomplish the things you need to do. Being overly busy is a sign that your life is out of balance. Following are five signs that your life is unbalanced:[2]

- *Busyness:* Are you always on the go and your house is in disarray? Do you always eat in your car or at your desk? Are you always in a hurry? Are you always running late?

- *Stress:* Do you have trouble sleeping at night or always feel anxious? Are you irritable with others? Do you have trouble making decisions?

- *Guilt:* Often when you're too busy, important things fall by the wayside. And the knowledge of all the things you aren't doing makes you feel guilty.

- *Escape:* Busyness often leads to seeking ways to escape

the daily grind; however, we can overcompensate and our choice of escape is often unhealthy. This can include impulsive spending, expensive vacations, overeating, excessive TV watching, or scrolling endlessly on Facebook. In the extreme, some people even turn to drugs or excessive alcohol consumption.

• *Spiritual deficit:* Time with God often suffers when you are always on the go. You may fail to read your Bible daily or spend regular time with God in prayer. Your church attendance may even be reduced as you work on Sundays to finish the things you didn't do or catch up on the sleep you didn't get during the week.

Get Back in Balance

Ephesians 4:1 encourages us to live a life worthy of our calling. Whatever God has called you to do, align your priorities around that, and everything else will fall into place. As Jesus said, "But seek first the kingdom of God and His righteousness, and all these things shall be added to you" (Matthew 6:33 NKJV).

If you feel your life is out of balance, pray and ask God for guidance. Ask Him where your life is out of alignment and ask for assistance getting your priorities back in order. Balance does not mean equal time, but it does mean giving the correct amount of time to the right things. There may be times of extreme busyness and deadlines, but this shouldn't be the norm.

Priorities can be divided into four broad categories: God, family, work, and self. God must always be first and foremost in our lives. When we neglect time with Him, every other area of our life will spin out of control. Many people find it hardest to balance life in the area of self. So many things take up your time that it almost feels selfish to take time for yourself. But sometimes it's necessary. You must take care of yourself, because you're the only one who can do so effectively. It is only in taking care of yourself that you have enough left over to give everyone else. Caring for yourself can include exercise, sleep, alone time, indulgence in hobbies, and prayer/meditation. Health is often the number one thing sacrificed as we try to tend to other things in our lives that seem more important.

It's important to distinguish between priorities and demands. Priorities are those things that are important to you, whereas demands are those things that are important to other people for you to do. Evaluate your day-to-day activities and determine how much of what you do is for other people and how much is in service of your life's priorities. If you are wondering how to restore balance to your life, here are some steps to get you there:[3]

1. Evaluate your time. You can't fix a problem if you don't know where the problem exists. Track your time for one week to determine how and where you are spending it. This activity can be quite illuminating, and it can help you plan your next steps.

2. Determine your priorities. Now that you know where you are spending your time, ask yourself whether the time spent lines up with your priorities. Often where we spend our time and what we say are priorities don't match. Ask yourself the following questions: "Is there anything I need to start doing? Is there anything I need to stop doing? Is there anything I need to do differently?"

3. Set goals. Armed with the information above, it's time to set goals. Use your list of priorities to set measurable goals.

4. Use a planner and spend some time with it each night to plan for the next day. This will help ensure that your priorities are established and at the front of your mind.

5. Establish boundaries. It's almost inevitable that when you set priorities, someone or something will come along to challenge them. This is why it's so important to have boundaries and stick to them. If you've decided you can't work overtime on Tuesdays and Thursdays because of your gym class, don't cave in every time you're asked. If you've made it clear you can't work on Sundays because you

reserve that time to go to church, firmly but gently explain that you won't be able to come in.

6. Take care of your health. If you are not in good health, you will have trouble managing your priorities. This is one of the most important things you can do for yourself. Make sure you have a regular exercise schedule, at least three times a week, and that you eat healthy meals. Make sure you get enough rest—most people need at least seven hours each night. Pay attention to your body to determine how much sleep you need. Avoid relying on alcohol or drugs to take the edge off. Taking care of yourself will decrease your stress levels, increase your energy and stamina, and improve your mental clarity. Overall you will be a happier person.

7. Nurture your relationships. Personal relationships can be deeply satisfying, but we often let them suffer when we are too busy. Make time for your friends and family. Don't be too busy when it's time for family gatherings. Go to dinner with your friends. Attend birthday parties. Yes, sometimes you really can't make certain activities, but this shouldn't be the norm when it comes to those you care for.

8. Make time for yourself. Be sure to include time in your schedule for personal fulfillment. Put your "me time" in your planner just like you would anything else important to you. Do you have a favorite TV show to watch every week? Write it down. Set aside the time if you enjoy reading before bed at night. Whatever hobby you have, be sure to include it in your daily activities.

9. Clock out of work. Leave your work at the office, both mentally and physically. When you leave work, put it out of your mind and focus on other areas of your life. If you work from home, this may be more difficult. Set business hours just as you would if you were working outside of

the house. If you've chosen 6:00 p.m. as the time to be off work, make sure you stop as soon as the clock strikes six. It's too easy to end up working at all times of day just because you can, but you will be more productive if you set work hours and stick to them. Late night hours should not be your norm.

10. Make use of time-management tools. With all the technology and tools available today, there's really no excuse not to manage your time wisely. At the very least, you need a planner, which you will use to turn your priorities and goals into reality. There are many different technology tools to help you manage your time, schedule events on a calendar, and help you set important reminders. You can use the calendar in your Google account, which can sync to your phone. There are also online time- and event-managing tools such as *Trello.com* and *Asana.com*.

You've worked hard for your success; don't allow it to be derailed by mismanaging your time. If you're still working toward your goals, prepare for your success by implementing what you've learned here. Don't allow busyness to distract you. Set boundaries with your loved ones, and pray for the courage to say no to those things that don't fall in line with your priorities.

PAY IT FORWARD

I n her 1999 novel *Pay It Forward*, Catherine Ryan Hyde tells the story of 12-year-old Trevor McKinney, who decides to accept his teacher's challenge to come up with a plan to change the world. Wanting the extra class credit, Trevor's plan is simple but transformational. He wants people to perform an act of kindness for three people, and rather than allowing them to return the favor, he wants them to ask the recipients to "pay it forward" (versus "pay it back") by extending an act of kindness to three other people. He envisions such generosity igniting fires of goodwill and kindness that will spread around the world. Indeed, it did. The book was adapted to a movie with the same title in 2000, and the lives of millions of readers and audiences were forever changed.

We have all been the recipient of somebody's benevolence, whether it was their time, their talent, or their treasure. While we are grateful, we are sometimes at a loss at to how to return the kindness, how to pay our benefactor back in some way. When we are the benefactor, a higher approach to expecting to be repaid for our kindness by the same person would be to encourage the recipient to "pay it forward" by blessing another person in similar circumstances.

The concept of "paying it forward" is about reaping and sowing—in that order. It's about acknowledging the benefit you have reaped from another and then planting that seed in someone else and seeing them impacted. Perhaps David had this concept in mind when he asked, "What shall I render to the LORD for all His benefits toward me?" (Psalm 116:12 NKJV). This mind-set requires us to do a bit of tweaking as we generally have focused on giving to others and then reaping a blessing for having done so.

Hall of Benefactors

I'm challenging you now to think about the people who invested their time pouring wisdom into you. The list may be short, but we have all stood on the shoulders of somebody to get to the next level— spiritually, emotionally, physically, relationally, or financially.

I'm eternally grateful for the mentorship of a few not-so-well-known spiritual giants. Lady Jean Mitchell, my pastor's wife during my college days at the University of North Texas, taught me the power of a simple "Help me, Lord" prayer when my boyfriend since ninth grade was killed in a car accident during my junior year. Since then, I've paid it forward and taught others how to be spiritually and emotionally strong in tough times by receiving God's peace that surpasses our understanding.

The late Dr. Marlene Talley cautioned me to adopt a oneness (instead of a "mine versus yours") mind-set toward the finances in my marriage and to always honor my husband with my words. I share these principles with married couples on a regular basis as my husband and I explain the power of financial intimacy and how to achieve it.

The late Dr. Juanita Smith taught me by example how to forgive and let go of a desire to retaliate when I've been wronged or offended. Her admonition to always declare "I release everybody" has been heard around the world as I've discussed it via global media outlets. Equally important, she encouraged me to refrain from using the phrase "you should" when giving input to anyone, especially my husband, and instead say, "Have you considered…?" Such an approach takes me out of the "mother" or "judge" seat and makes the hearer more receptive.

I've made every effort to pay it forward in each of these instances. Think of the people whose wisdom helped to shape your destiny. Consider ways that you can pay it forward if you have not done so already.

Faithful over a Few Things; Ruler over Much

It may not seem relevant, but often someone's lack of generosity can be the very roadblock to getting a project off the ground. Take the case of Vera, who has sought to launch her business for the past ten years. She has a unique product with a solid patent. Several huge corporations have expressed interest in her venture, but each negotiation has resulted in a dead end. She has maxed out her credit cards living above her means, boasting that the "big deal" is just around the corner.

Many people have sown into her effort. Her sister is a popular business consultant and has spent hours counseling Vera on how to structure deals with investors, how to select the right operating executives for the company, and so forth. Yet she has never expressed her gratitude or even sent her a birthday card. She never donates to a charity when there is a national disaster. Rather, she declares, "When my business gets off the ground, I'll write checks for thousands of dollars to family, charities, and others."

Vera believes her rhetoric—but she has yet to grasp the principle of sowing and reaping! Oh, she admits she has reaped many benefits from the hands of others; unfortunately, she finds sowing problematic. None of the spiritually sober people in her circle can convince her that the best strategy is to start her charitable efforts right now—right at her current level of income. The truth is that how we manage limited funds is the best indication of how we will manage abundance. Jesus said so: "If you are faithful in little things, you will be faithful in large ones" (Luke 16:10 NLT). Could it be that Vera's refusal to sow into others is holding up her business success?

Practical Ways to Pay It Forward

Perhaps it's time for you to pay it forward. Here are a few suggestions to get you started.

- Return someone's meanness with a smile; tell a rude clerk, "Things will get better. Hang in there."
- Leave an encouraging note or affirmation for your boss or employee highlighting a professional attribute or behavior

that you respect. (Example: "I really respect your quest for excellence in everything you do.")

- Send an appreciation card to your pastor, your loyal friend, the neighbor who keeps an eye on your property when you travel, or anyone who extends a kindness or benefit to you.

- Donate something you really like (or that you recently purchased) to a charity.

- Be sensitive to those who serve or work for you domestically or in business. Give the gardener a cold drink on a hot day; give your housekeeper a few dollars more than her customary fee; bring in a healthy snack to the office to share with all.

- Let someone go ahead of you at the bank, grocery store, or other places where people stand in line.

- Tip your food server more than the standard 15 percent.

- Put money in a parking meter that has expired. (This one backfired on me after I put several quarters at different intervals in an expired meter where a Rolls Royce was parked in downtown Los Angeles. When the owner finally appeared, I couldn't resist telling him I'd saved him from getting a ticket. He informed me that he had a handicap decal and was exempt from putting money in the meter!)

- Keep a stash of dollar bills handy in your car to help homeless people on the street.

The Supreme Supplier

God has promised to supply all of our needs according to His riches in glory (Philippians 4:19). I can't close this book without sharing how one generous couple paid it forward and miraculously met Chrissy's need. Here is how she related the story to me:

A couple of years ago I had an urgent need for $10,000 within the next 30 days. I tried to figure out how to make that amount of money quickly, but I kept drawing blanks. Finally, I wrote down the need in my journal, cried, prayed, and let it go. A few days later, a good friend called and said that she and her husband had prayed for me a few nights earlier. She said they were selling their house, which a family member had paid off as a gift to them. They were going to have at least $200,000 at their disposal, and the Lord told them to give me $10,000. I couldn't believe it! It took them about a month to sell the house. The day they wired the money to me was the very day I needed it. I will never, ever forget God's faithfulness.

Yes, God supplies according to *His* riches. There is no need for us to analyze and agonize over the adequacy of our resources when the Supreme Supplier is our Father.

YOUR FINANCIAL MANIFESTO

1. In obedience to God, I faithfully pay my tithes, give offerings, and help those in need.

2. I take full responsibility for where I stand financially.

3. I forgive and release all who have ever financially disadvantaged me in any way.

4. I do not allow my net worth to define my self-worth.

5. I refuse to enable irresponsible people to continue their negative financial behavior.

6. I walk in integrity in all my financial dealings.

7. I maintain a healthy balance between saving for the future and enjoying my blessings today.

8. I reject a scarcity mentality and choose to help others achieve their goals by sharing my knowledge, experiences, contacts, and other resources.

9. I continually seek to increase my knowledge of financial concepts and strategies.

10. I look to God as my Supreme Financial Adviser and the Supplier of all of my needs.

BALANCE SHEET TEMPLATE

What I Own and What I Owe as of _____

Assets (What I Own)	(Fair Market Value)
Cash in Banks	
Stocks and Bonds	
Cash Value: Life Insurance Policy	
Jewelry/Art/Clothing	
Vehicles	
House/Condo	
Rental Property	
Other:	
Other:	
Total Assets	
Liabilities: (What I Owe)	**(Fair Market Value)**
Credit Card #1:	
Credit Card #2:	
Credit Card #3:	
Auto Loan	
Mortgage Loan	
School Loan	
Other:	
Other:	
Total Liabilities	
Net Worth (Assets minus Liabilities)	
Total Liabilities and Net Worth	

STATEMENT OF CASH RECEIPTS AND DISBURSEMENTS TEMPLATE

What I Get and Where It Goes

Take Home Income (After Taxes):	
Source 1:	
Source 2:	
Total Income	
Less: Charitable Donations	
Less: Savings	
Net Cash Available	
FIXED EXPENSES	
Rent/Mortgage	
Auto Loan/Bus Fare	
Auto Insurance	
Credit Card Payments (minimum)	
Water/Gas	
Electricity	
Medical/Life Insurance	
Total Fixed Expenses	
VARIABLE EXPENSES:	
Auto Repairs/Maintenance	
Lunches	
Groceries	
Recreation/Cable	

Laundry/Dry Cleaning	
Telephone	
Gasoline	
Clothing	
Grooming (Hair, Nails, etc.)	
Vacation Reserve	
Other:	
Total Variable Expenses	
TOTAL ALL EXPENSES	
NET EXCESS (DEFICIT) CASH	

FINANCIAL EMPOWERMENT RESOURCES

- Top personal finance sites (timely articles, how-tos): *www.bankrate.com, CNNmoney.com, MoneyCentral.msn.com*

- Free copy of your credit report (annually) from the three reporting agencies— Equifax, Experian, and TransUnion (does not include your FICO score; see below): *http://www.annualcreditreport.com/*

- Copy of your FICO credit score (not free): *www.MyFico.com.*

- Advice about a variety of credit card issues from top experts: *https://www.creditcards.com*

- Life insurance calculator (determine how much coverage you need): *http://money.msn.com/life-insurance/life -insurance-quotes.aspx, http://www.insure.com/articles/ interactivetools/lifeneedsestimator/calculate.jsp*

- Life insurance quotes: *www.selectquote.com, www.zanderinsurance.co*m

- Quicken WillMaker Plus (software for preparing wills): *http://www.nolo.com/products/quicken-willmaker-plus-wqp .html*

- Living trust templates (for wills, trusts, power of attorney, advance directives, etc.): *https://store.nolo.com/products /online-living-trust-nntrus.html, www.suzeorman willandtrust.com*

- Copy of your personal Social Security statement: *http://www.ssa.gov/myaccount*

- Funding your child's education: *www.SavingForCollege.com*

- Investing 101: A Tutorial for Beginner Investors: *https://www.investopedia.com/university/beginner/*

- Trustworthy, established discount brokerage houses for purchasing stocks and bonds: *Vanguard.com, Fidelity.com, Schwab.com*

- Guide to finding fee-based financial advisors: *Napfa.org, GarrettPlanningNetwork.com*

- Financial calculators (various financial calculators for auto loans, mortgages, student loans, investments, income taxes, and other): *http://www.financialcalculator.org*

- Guideline and tips for buying and selling cars: *https://www.edmunds.com/*

- Options and alternatives for repaying federal student loans: *http://studentaid.ed.gov/repay-loans*

- "How to Review Your New Car Sales Contract": *https://www.edmunds.com/car-buying/how-to-review-your -new-car-sales-contract.html*

NOTES

Chapter 2

1. Cameron Huddleston, "69% of Americans Have Less Than $1,000 in Savings," Go Banking Rates, September 19, 2016, www.gobankingrates.com/personal-finance/data-americans-savings.

Chapter 4

1. Adapted from Deborah Smith Pegues, *30 Days to Taming Your Finances* (Eugene, OR: Harvest House Publishers, 2006), 154.

Chapter 5

1. Howard Dayton, "Are You Financially Bound?" Crosswalk.com, September 21, 2007, https://www.crosswalk.com/family/finances/are-you-financially-bound-11554830.html.

Chapter 7

1. Sabah Karimi, "6 Danger Signs of Emotional Spending," U.S. News and World Report, May 21, 2014, https://money.usnews.com/money/blogs/my-money/2014/05/21/6-danger-signs-of-emotional-spending.

Chapter 9

1. Ruth Umoh, "How Overcoming the Fear of Failure Helped Steve Jobs, Tim Ferriss and Bill Gates Succeed," CNBC.com, August 7, 2017, https://www.cnbc.com/2017/08/07/how-overcoming-the-fear-of-failure-helped-steve-jobs-and-bill-gates.html.

2. Bill Gates, *Business @ the Speed of Thought* (New York: Warner Books, 1999), 184.

3. Umoh, "How Overcoming the Fear of Failure Helped Steve Jobs, Tim Ferriss and Bill Gates Succeed," CNBC.com, August 7, 2017, https://www.cnbc.com/2017/08/07/how-overcoming-the-fear-of-failure-helped-steve-jobs-and-bill-gates.html.

4. Peter Jones, "How Oprah Winfrey Overcame Failure," The Job Network, accessed November 28, 2018, https://www.thejobnetwork.com/how-oprah-winfrey-overcame-failure.

5. Steve Pavlina, "Fear of Success: What Will Happen If You Succeed?" StevePavlina.com (blog), December 4, 2004, https://www.stevepavlina.com/blog/2004/12/fear-of-success-what-will-happen-if-you-succeed.

Chapter 16

1. Holden Lewis, "Which Mortgage Is Right for You? Comparing Conventional, FHA and VA Loans," Bankrate.com, January 15, 2018, www.bankrate.com/finance/mortgages/conventional-fha-va-mortgage.aspx.

2. Polyana Da Costa, "5 Things to Know About Getting a VA Loan," Bankrate.com, January 17, 2017, https://www.bankrate.com/finance/mortgages/getting-va-loan.aspx.

Chapter 18

1. "The State of Women-Owned Businesses Report," http://about.americanexpress.com/news/docs/2017-State-of-Women-Owned-Businesses-Report.pdf.

Chapter 20

1. Nicholas Pell, "The 5 Basic Insurance Policies Everyone Should Have," Mint.com, February 6, 2013, https://blog.mint.com/planning/the-5-basic-insurance-policies-everyone-should-have-0213/.

2. "How Much Will Life Insurance Cost Me?" CNN Money, accessed December 7, 2017, http://money.cnn.com/retirement/guide/insurance_life.moneymag/index9.htm.

3. Dave Ramsey, "After the Divorce: How to Secure Your Financial Future," accessed December 8, 2017, https://www.daveramsey.com/blog/after-the-divorce-get-financial-feet-back.

Chapter 21

1. Jane Collingwood, "Learning to Say No," Psych Central, July 17, 2016, https://psychcentral.com/lib/learning-to-say-no/.

2. Chip Ingram, "Are Your Priorities in Balance?" Living on the Edge with Chip Ingram, January 15, 2014, https://livingontheedge.org/read-blog/blog/2014/01/16/are-your-priorities-in-balance-.

3. Tim Kehl, "12 Key Strategies to Achieving a Work-Life Balance," Industry Week, April 18, 2012, http://www.industryweek.com/leadership/12-key-strategies-achieving-work-life-balance.

Acknowledgments

Thanks to my heavenly Father, who never gives me a responsibility without giving me the ability to respond.

Thanks to all the women who shared their financial experiences, fears, and aspirations with me. Your participation has added value to other women in ways you will never know.

Thanks to my Harvest House team for their patience with all my life circumstances that threatened the completion of the manuscript. Your care, concern, and commitment to the Word put you in a special class of publishers.

Thanks to my research assistant, Cynthia Tucker, for her diligence in researching many aspects of the book. Also, the informal critiques from numerous personal and social media friends were a real godsend. I'm grateful to you all.

Thanks to my incredible husband, Darnell Pegues, for his efforts to help me stay focused on writing while also providing for times of rest and refreshment from the process.

Thanks to my friends who maintained our relationship despite the fact that I never seemed to be available during this extended project. I appreciate all of you and promise to make it up to you.

Thanks to my intercessory prayer warriors for the doing the "real" work that brought this project to fruition. You know who you are and, most importantly, God knows and will reward you according to your kindness.

About the Author

Deborah Smith Pegues is a CPA/MBA, TV host, certified John Maxwell Leadership Coach, certified behavior consultant, Bible teacher, and global speaker. She has written 16 transformational books, including the bestselling *30 Days to Taming Your Tongue* (over one million sold) and *Emergency Prayers*. She and her husband, Darnell, have been married since 1979 and reside in Southern California.

To contact the author:

E-mail: Deborah@ConfrontingIssues.com

Website: www.ConfrontingIssues.com

(323) 293-5861

Other Books by Deborah Smith Pegues

30 Days to Taming Your Tongue

30 Days to Taming Your Tongue Workbook

30 Days to Taming Worry and Anxiety

30 Days to Taming Your Fears

30 Days to Taming Your Finances

30 Days to Taming Your Anger

30 Days to Taming Your Emotions

30 Days to Taming Your Kid's Tongue

Emergency Prayers

Why Smart People Make Dumb Choices

30 Days to a Stronger, More Confident You

Choose Your Attitude, Change Your Life

Confronting Without Offending

Forgive, Let Go, and Live

Socially Confident in 60 Seconds